BEING THE
STARFISH™

Being the Starfish^{TM}*: 7 Steps to Sharing So People Want to Buy*
by Neal Anderson

All Scripture quotes, unless otherwise noted, are taken from the English Standard Version.

ISBN-13:978-1505495485
ISBN-10:1505495482

For additional information or bulk discount program please visit our website at www.shareleadinspire.com

Printed in the United States of America

BEING THE
STARFISH™

7 STEPS TO SHARING
SO PEOPLE *WANT* TO BUY

NEAL ANDERSON

CONTENTS

THE STARFISH™ CREED

Love is patient and kind; love does not envy or boast; it is not arrogant or rude. It does not insist on its own way; it is not irritable or resentful; it does not rejoice at wrongdoing, but rejoices with the truth. Love bears all things, believes all things, hopes all things, endures all things.

—1 Corinthians 13:4–7

CHAPTER 1

FROM BUCKETS TO PIPELINES: BUILDING A BETTER WAY

Your success and significance in life will be in direct proportion to the number of times you put others and yourself in a position to hear yes or no.

—Neal Anderson

Big disclaimer: I am not on the New York Times Bestseller list. I do not have a fancy publisher (my editor and compositor are awesome, though).

I've been through tens of thousands of noes to get where I am today. I know what it's like to have a door slammed in my face, to be rejected, to be alone. But each time, I picked myself up and focused on finding a way instead of an excuse.

My first introduction to the world of sales (besides trying to sell my way with my parents beginning at age two) was as a ten-year-old living in upstate New York. The local YMCA had a free throw shooting contest, with a free membership going to the winner. Kids would knock on doors for a month to get folks to pledge a certain amount for every free throw a kid could make in a fifteen-minute period.

I knocked on every door I could find, often past dark. Some enthusiastic neighbors pledged up to twenty-five cents per successful shot. I filled up page after page with generous pledges. Then came the time to shoot the free throws.

Some would say I was a good little basketball player. I practiced nonstop in every driveway on the street. As the neighborhood's youngest player, I had to either suck it up or get beat.

Free throws were easy for me—so easy that I ended up making 149 in fifteen minutes and beat all of the high school kids and YMCA counselors.

Then came the time to collect the pledges. For fear of bankrupting our neighbors, my dad wrote a letter explaining my success and inviting people to give whatever they felt led to give instead of their committed pledge.

That was my first experience with setting a goal, selling an idea, and then getting exactly what I pictured. I knew I was going to win.

After a nineteen-year retirement, I ran up to my first house again. This time I was in eastern Tennessee selling reference books and software door-to-door to pay my way through college and law school. For six hot summers, I knocked on doors and shared my ideas with people from all walks of life, socioeconomic backgrounds, and dialects. It was here that I learned how to be a STARfish™ instead of a SELLfish™.

Later I was an account executive, selling law books and web-based libraries to law firms for an international legal publishing company. I've sold everything from books door-to-door, to high-end real estate, to clinical-grade sleep systems—to dōTERRA®! I've made over 50,000 sales calls and performed over 5,500 presentations in living rooms across the country. Add to that another 5,000 presentations in law offices and boardrooms during my eleven-year corporate career.

Yet after all my years of experience in many different industries, I have yet to see anything like dōTERRA. What a blessing we all have!

In my previous occupations, although I was getting invaluable experience and making great money, I was building someone else's company, someone else's dream. And I was sacrificing mine.

I was sick of starting at zero every day, month, and year. Finally it dawned on me—a transforming insight: *I was hauling buckets instead of building a pipeline.*

ARE YOU BUILDING A PIPELINE OR HAULING BUCKETS?

In his book *Rich Dad's Cashflow* Quadrant, Robert Kiyosaki wrote about a man who carried buckets of water from a creek to a small town every day. He made this trip multiple times per day and could only increase his income if he hauled more buckets. The man had plenty of job security because the town needed a daily supply of water.

Then one day another man also started carrying buckets. Facing competition, the first man knew there was only one way to increase the amount of water he could provide: build a pipeline from the creek to the town. So he figured out how much money he needed to live on as well as pay for supplies to build the pipeline, and he used his spare time to build the pipeline.

Day after day, the first man hauled the requisite number of buckets to cover his expenses, and then he worked on the pipeline.

The second man meanwhile continued to haul bucket after bucket into the little town, ultimately hauling more water than the first man.

After two years, the first man finally completed his pipeline. His first customer turned on the faucet and out came clean, cold water. Excited townspeople lined up, eager to purchase. All they had to do was turn on the faucet. Soon there were no lines, because people could get the first man's water whenever they desired.

The man realized he had built not only a physical pipeline to carry more water but also a financial pipeline which would enable him to leverage his time, treasure, and passions.

I love this story because it demonstrates how powerful owning a business can be for a family as well as that family's community.

Day after day, schools and universities promote the bucket-hauling mindset at the expense of people's dreams. Countless men and women get good grades, go to college, get a job, and then think they will retire on a nice income. Unfortunately, the days when that approach worked are long gone. Yet our educational factories are still tooled for it.

Back when I was hauling buckets uphill every day for the legal research company, I annually sold almost a million dollars of subscriptions, and year after year I woke up on the first of January sitting on zero. I had to start all over again. Of all those millions in sales I had made, I never saw a shred of continuing return. My livelihood depended on my constantly pumping out new subscriptions.

If I stopped working the next day, my pay would stop. (Indeed, the last I heard from the company was when they mailed me my final paycheck—two weeks after I "retired.") That's when it hit me: I was hauling buckets.

One day I added up all the reoccurring revenue I had ever produced. I looked at how many customers had purchased from me. And I wondered: What if I had my own business, and my customers could be paying *me*, not someone else!

I wanted to leverage my time, my talents, and my treasures. I wanted to serve people a few times very well and get paid as they enjoyed the benefits of purchasing the products over and over. And that is what started my quest to build my pipeline instead of hauling buckets. Thankfully, dōTERRA found my wife and me, and the bucket hauling has been replaced by a pipeline of wellness and financial freedom.

A BETTER WAY

According to Gallup.Com, approximately 70 percent of workers feel disengaged from their work, and a high percentage want to be doing something else. This has to change. Too many people are working too many hours for too many companies that provide little opportunity to create a great lifestyle—one that empowers people to fulfill their calling *and* spend more time with their families. The current work environment often takes people away from both their families and their dreams.

I am grateful that my wife and I have found a better way (or it found us). It's one that enables us to serve people in a manner I believe God designed us for. Yet misconceptions abound about network marketing, aka multilevel marketing (MLM). And rightly so.

At a large dōTERRA leadership retreat I attended, full of Silver rank and above, the speaker asked the audience, "How many of you said you would never do network marketing?" By my estimate, 99 percent of the room raised their hands. How about you? What was *your* opinion of network marketing before you discovered dōTERRA?

People's perceptions are often shaped by all of the opportunity-peddlers who promote fancy cars and dream lifestyles rather than allowing the products and the retention rate to stand on their own merits. Too often, when people realize that the opportunity was unequally yoked with the product, the proverbial house of cards comes crashing down—along with years of trust and friendships.

At dōTERRA, we have the opportunity to share a blessing with people. And we do it the right way. We get to *share* instead of sell. To *sow* instead of constantly feeling like we have to hoodwink the next person we see into joining a pie-in-the-sky opportunity. dōTERRA is not perfect nor is it for everyone. But one thing is for sure: dōTERRA is about *giving* first without regard to what we may receive in the end.

There is an old saying: "Nothing happens until someone sells something." The problem with that expression is, selling is the focus. The motive is often to achieve a quota, win a trip or a car, or appease a pest of an upline leader. What happens to ethics and culture when production is the priority?

Imagine if, instead, our primary goal was to understand others and help them get that which will improve their life's significance.

Sharing is about being more concerned for others than you are for yourself, your company, or your bank account. When we break off a piping hot piece of our chocolate chip cookie and hand it to a friend, we do it not to win a contest, gain a promotion, or get a sale. We do it because we love this specific chocolate chip cookie experience, and we want to share it with someone else who we feel would love it as much as we do. Our intention is not to *sell* it but to *share it.* That is being a STARfish.

There are many ways to get from point A to point B in hopes that someone will come to our way of thinking and believing. We believe that our product can help someone. We believe that our product is the best option. But how do we persuade others without putting pressure on them or scaring them away?

This book will show you how, and show you well. In *Being the STARfish: 7 Steps to Sharing So People Want to Buy,* you will discover the difference between a *STARfish* and a *SELLfish* and identity a path to your calling. You will gain insight into the value of your time and learn how to accomplish everything you dream of with less stress. You will learn how people buy and how to "control the controllables." Finally, you will walk through the 10 steps of the Share Cycle™, from fishing for people to inspiring a roomful of future wellness advocates.

I am optimistic that a new day has dawned, and the stale tactics and motivations so common to this profession will soon give way to a mission that has one purpose: helping people access products that change their lives, so they can love God and others abundantly.

You are going to have to work hard doing something for the next three to five years. You might as well work at building *your* dream and your business instead of someone else's.

My wish for you is that you will read this book with an open heart and simply believe you are worth it. Please use your God-given gifts, talents, and treasures to serve people the way God intended you to do. People are counting on you.

THE MAN IN THE ARENA

It is not the critic who counts; not the man who points out how the strong man stumbles, or where the doer of deeds could have done them better. The credit belongs to the man who is actually in the arena, whose face is marred by dust and sweat and blood: who strives valiantly; who errs, who comes short again and again, because there is no effort without error and shortcoming; but who does actually strive to do the deeds; who knows great enthusiasms, the great devotions; who spends himself in a worthy cause; who at the worst, if he fails, at least fails while daring greatly, so that his place shall never be with those cold and timid souls who neither know victory nor defeat.

—Theodore Roosevelt

CHAPTER 2

BEING THE STARFISH™

They are to do good, to be rich in good works,
to be generous and ready to share.
—1 Timothy 6:18

Sellfy the SELLfish was giddy with excitement. His very first
network marketing company! He couldn't wait to get started.
Granted, he felt a little nervous, but he thought, "How hard
can it be? I'm a good talker and I'm *great* with people."

Out Sellfy charged, beating the bushes for enrollees in his hot
new opportunity. No need to use the company material—why
bother. Sellfy had confidence. Charisma. A great product. He'd do
things his way.

But an astonishing thing happened: people weren't interested.
How could that be?

"Maybe I need to know everything before people will listen to
me," Sellfy thought. So he started memorizing the oil books, learning
the chemistry of Vetiver and other essential oils. And day after day
he hit the local coffee shops to study his oil books and uncover a hot
prospect. But no luck. People weren't buying.

So it went for two discouraging weeks—and then, suddenly, inspiration hit. Social media! Surely that was the key. Why hadn't he thought of it before! With renewed vigor, Sellfy blasted Facebook, Twitter, and Instagram with specials and deals, hoping to lure someone, anyone, into hearing his pitch.

Still no good. No one wanted to talk to him.

Sellfy's confidence and enthusiasm were dropping like thermometer mercury in an arctic blast. Finally, discouraged and at his wit's end, he decided to talk with one of the company's top wellness advocates.

Sherri the STARfish had a bounce in her step and a great attitude, and she always seemed *happy*. She also had a large team of customers and business partners. In her office, Sellfy poured out his frustration. "Sherri, I've been miserable," he confessed. "I'm trying my hardest, but no one wants what I have. I just don't get it. Is my town saturated? Is it a bad time of year? Is it because of my upline leader?"

"Sellfy, did you pay attention to your team's training?" Sherri asked gently.

"I didn't go. I figured it was all a bunch of hype, so I skipped it. Did you go, Sherri?"

"Of course I did."

"What did they cover?" Now Sellfy was genuinely curious.

"The presenters taught us how to succeed by using duplicable systems. They also said that many people would try to wing it, try to do it their own way, and those people would get frustrated. They told us to not reinvent the wheel but trust the systems. Things would go better that way, and if we did a few things right, we would be successful."

Sherri talked about sharing instead of selling. About how people love to buy but dislike being sold. About the difference between being a STARfish instead of a SELLfish.

"SELLfish focus on selling and on getting what they can get instead of giving what they can give," Sherri said. "They have a heart of scarcity instead of abundance. They complain about things that are out of their control, and they're usually the first ones to brag about a rank or company car they want to win. They also focus on their own needs instead of the customer's needs, and they usually wing it when faced with using a system."

Sellfy winced. *Bullseye.*

Sherri continued. "SELLfish create a high-pressure selling environment. They fail to take corrective criticism when there is room for improvement. They don't understand how people buy, and they usually overpromise and underdeliver."

Sherri smiled. "There's another, much more fruitful way."

"And that is?"

"Being a STARfish. Someone who focuses on sowing, on giving from a heart of abundance.

"STARfish control the controllables and focus on activity instead of results. They are extremely coachable. They focus on other people's needs, and they always use duplicable sharing systems and teach them to their team.

"STARfish create a sharing environment by letting people feel comfortable saying no if the products aren't a fit. They have learned how people like to be taken through the buying process in a way that puts everyone at ease. And they always *under*promise and *over*deliver."

Sherri leaned back in her chair and looked at Sellfy, and for a moment, there was silence.

Sellfy stared at the floor. "I've been doing everything all wrong," he finally said. "I've been so focused on myself that I haven't taken the time to figure out what the customer wants. I haven't been coachable.

And I've been doing way too much talking and not asking enough good questions in order to fully understand what people want."

"So how will you change that?"

"Honestly? I'm not sure how to go about it, Sherri."

"How about if I were to give you some personal coaching? I can walk you through a duplicable sharing process that will get you back on track. There's no reason why you can't fulfill your dream of helping people and being financially free. You just need a little guidance."

"Seriously? You'd do that for me?"

"Yes, Sellfy. I believe in you, and I know you can be extremely successful if you'll just do several basic things.

"But for starters, I want to address a few matters so you can have the very best experience.

"Here is what you can count on from me. First, I will always believe in you. When you tell me that you want to reach a certain rank, or hold five classes a month, or whatever goal you set, I'm going to believe you can do it.

"Second, I will always be positive. I know how tough it can be to talk to people and not always get the result you hope for. So you need to know that I will be your biggest cheerleader.

"Third, Sellfy, I'll always level with you. I will tell you what you need to hear, not what you want to hear. This is for your benefit, not mine.

"Fourth, I will never ask you to do anything I'm not doing or haven't done a million times.

"There are only six things it takes to prosper in our business. If you do them, then you will succeed and help a lot of people in the process. This isn't magic. It's a formula. It's a system, and when you learn the system, you will live your dream.

"You can either work with human nature or against it. This system will help you work with it.

"So if you want to be not only successful but also significant, here is what I need to count on from you. First, I need you to be extremely coachable. When I ask you to read a book or attend a meeting or learn a technique, you have to trust that I won't recommend anything unless it will help you a ton. Maybe one of my suggestions will strike you as silly or unnecessary. Please trust me that it works and do it anyway. Remember, you don't need to *feel* like doing something in order to do it!

"Second, I need to count on you to always be positive. Positive around other teammates, positive with customers, positive at home, and positive in classes. Your attitude will determine your altitude.

"Third, I need to count on your working hard. When your schedule says it's time to work on your business, I need to trust that you'll do so. You'll make the calls, invite the people, and do the classes. I promise, the enrollments will take care of themselves if you do your best.

"Fourth, I need you to study hard. Study your scripts, study your products, and make sure you are a student of this business.

"Fifth, I need to count on you to always level with me. Let me know what is really going on. That is the only way I can help you. You can always talk to me. One thing we do on our team is this: If you're having a bad moment—we don't have bad days—you simply "puke up." Up, okay? Never across or down. If you have an issue with something, call me and we will work it out. Don't call someone below you on the team or someone on another team. Just call me. I promise we can work it out and find a solution.

"But before you call me, whether it's about an issue or with a question, I want you to ask yourself three things: What is the situation?

What are my options? And what do I think I should do? I'll bet that most of the time, you will find the solution yourself. If you need another opinion once you've gone through the questions, then call me and tell me which option you feel would be the best.

"Finally, be someone who finds a way instead of an excuse. You will be tempted to make excuses—because anything worth anything involves hard work, frustration, and persistence. You may want to give up. But you are going to be the type of person who finds a way.

"Can I count on you to do these six things, Sellfy?"

"You bet!"

"Excellent! Because if you do, then you will get where you want to go.

"Now, one last question: Can I hold you accountable to do all of these things the best you can?"

With a grin, Sellfy shook Sherri's hand and looked her in the eye. "I'm all in," he said.

CHAPTER 3

YOUR WHY
YOUR INTENTION
YOUR CALLING

*It is God who is producing in you both the desire
and the ability to do what pleases him.*
—Philippians 2:13 ISV

I n his excellent book *Start with Why*, Simon Sinek made the case that people don't care about what you do. They care why you do it. Yet many of us in sales communicate in terms of *what*—what products we sell and how one feature or benefit is better than another—while failing to ever let people know *why* we are doing what we do. Yet if that question goes unanswered, our prospects are unlikely to connect emotionally with our *cause*. And it's that emotional connection that creates customers.

Most people in a company or organization know *what* they do, says Sinek. Fewer people know *how* they do it. (For example, a person in the shipping department may not understand the complete manufacturing process.) And very few in most organizations know *why* their company does what it does, which may explain the low level of employee engagement which Gallup perennially reports.

Sinek illustrates the what/how/why concept and its ramifications graphically with his "Golden Circle": three concentric circles which show how most companies communicate. The outer circle is what a company does; the next circle is how the company does it, and the inner circle is why.

Most people and organizations communicate from the outer ring and work their way in. For example: "We sell essential oils (What). We teach classes about their benefits (How). Do you want to buy some (Why)?" Not very inspiring.

But what if we reverse that order and communicate from the inside out, starting with Why, as Sinek suggests. Now we're speaking to the emotional part of people's brain, where buying decisions are made. When we do that, we inspire people and help them feel excited about our cause—because they're experiencing us as a STARfish, not a SELLfish.

Here is how the conversation might go when you start with Why:

"In everything we do at dōTERRA, we believe in thinking differently. We challenge the status quo. (That's the Why.) The way we do this is by making natural products that are safer, cheaper, and more effective than traditional healthcare options. (You've just explained the How). We just happen to make wellness products. Would you like to buy some, or maybe come to a class to learn more about how they can help you? (Last of all, there's the What)."

You see the dramatic difference between leading with Why instead of What? Why is inspiring; What, on the other hand, is a turn-off when it's out of order.

THE INTENTION CYCLE™

People want to know your intention. They want to know what you believe. Why are you calling to invite them to a class? Is it only so you can make money off of them, or do you genuinely have their best interests in mind? For instance, do you care that they have the tools to provide their family with safe, effective, and affordable healthcare options?

The Intention Cycle™ shown here illustrates the relationship between your Why, which is central, and the sequence of relationship-building that your Why has the potential to generate, beginning with intention and culminating in enrollment.

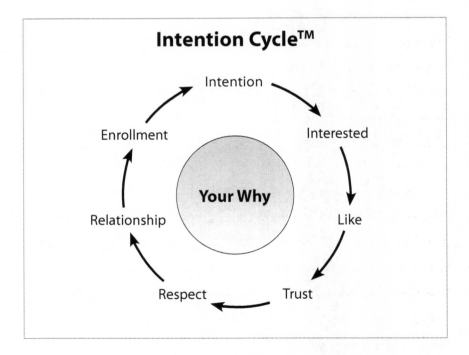

The Intention Cycle is integral to the STARfish way of life. When people know your intention, they become interested in you and in what you have to say. They begin to like you, and from there, they come to trust you, which leads to respecting you, which leads to a relationship. The fruit of that relationship *may* be an enrollment. If so, wonderful! But if not, that's okay, because you're dealing with a person you truly care about, not just a potential source of income.

This process can take seven seconds, seven minutes, seven days, or never. The sooner people know why you are doing what you do, the sooner you can help them obtain something that could change their lives. You've got to cultivate credibility before you talk about your products and how great they are. Otherwise, as you describe those products, what your prospects are mostly hearing is your lack of concern for them as people. Internally they're asking, "Do I trust this person?" "Is what they are saying even true?" "Why exactly are they inviting me to a class?" "What is their intention?"

Disregard for the Intention Cycle on the part of those in sales has left many people with a negative impression of our profession. They've tasted the SELLfish side of sales—but you can give them a better experience. Communicating your intention quickly will open up skeptical individuals to a whole new world of possibilities.

AWAKEN. DEEPEN. FULFILL.

In his book *It's Your Call*, Gary Barkalow writes, "What you were created to do is revealed in the form of your desires." Those desires, says Barkalow, unfold in a three-part pattern of awakening, deepening, and fulfillment.

God has a journey for every person, and that journey has many different paths, not just one. But every journey follows a similar trajectory: God *awakens* a desire in your heart, and you take a first step, and then another, and another.

As the journey progresses, you gain an education and experience, and you get better at what you do as a result. You're *deepening* your knowledge and ability—and the more proficient you get, the more satisfaction you experience in what you do and the more passionate you feel about it. Your Why is maturing.

Ultimately, God uses your perseverance and faithfulness to bring about the *fulfillment* of your original desire—and then he calls you higher by awakening you to something new, and you start all over.

Let's say, for example, that God stirs in you the desire to share dōTERRA. You deepen this desire by educating yourself, teaching classes, and serving customers. In time, you arrive at the point where your oils are paid for every month. You've gained knowledge and expertise, deepened your abilities as a presenter and educator, and perhaps now God awakens in you a new desire to build a team. Thus you acquire a new purpose, a new intention. Your Why begins to change.

YOUR PERSONAL WHY VERSUS THE CORPORATE WHY

Insightful though Simon Sinek's book is, its title, *Start with Why*, can be misleading unless we understand what Sinek means by it. So let's clarify an important point: the Why he has in mind is the corporate Why that drives an entire company, not the individual Why that drives you and me in what we do.

If all the people at Apple stopped making computers and started making jet skis, the jet skis they turned out wouldn't look anything like what we're used to. That's because Apple's corporate Why is to challenge the status quo and think differently, whether the product is computers or jet skis or a better mousetrap. Without that company intention, the workers would likely become disengaged.

But in sales, your prospects want to know your personal Why. And unlike the Why that motivates a company such as Apple, your Why is prone to change. This is because as you deepen your knowledge and experience, new possibilities open for you, and God awakens in you a desire to respond to those possibilities. Life is a constant revealing of new desires as you fulfill previous ones, and your Why modifies accordingly.

So although it's important to define the motive that drives what you do (and the exercises you'll be doing shortly will help you do just that), you should start with the following understanding. Underline it, circle it, and highlight it with a big orange marker: *You don't need to have your Why all figured out in order to get started at doing what you do.*

Action creates your Why, and that Why isn't static. It will evolve as you continue to act. So if you want to discover your Why, put yourself in motion. And bear this in mind: your Why is developed as you do things you don't feel like doing. Do them anyway. Out of them will emerge the passion you're looking for, the oil that fuels your torch. There are no shortcuts, and there is always pain in any beginning. But pressing on despite a lack of clarity will produce the clarity and purpose you desire.

Unfortunately, many people put the cart before the horse. Their Why-focus causes them to act only when they feel like it. And when they don't feel the burning passion of a Why, they do nothing—or worse, they make excuses. That's the danger of focusing inordinately on your Why: doing so can paralyze you when you need to be in motion, and just as bad, it can make you self-focused.

Loving God and serving people is the taproot of an awesome life; loving what you do is simply the fruit. Remember, it's not about you.

You will find your fulfillment as a result of deepening and fulfilling the desire that God puts in your heart.

With that said, it's important to understand what motivates you to do what you do. You need to understand your Why, and we're about to get into that. Let's begin with this understanding: The right kind of Why isn't defined merely by the things you think you want—that's too small a motive. *A Why worth living for is always about something bigger than you.*

One last word before the exercises: There's a difference between your Why and your calling. *Why* is about your intention for doing something, and it is prone to change. Your *calling*, on the other hand, involves the way God has wired you. It's something you can't turn off, and it is larger than any one occupation or job. Your Why forms in the process of doing something with increasing expertise, and fulfillment comes from doing it well. But your calling is a constant that resides in your heart.

DEFINE YOUR VISION/DEFINE YOUR CALLING

Take time to think through the following questions. Space is provided to write down your answers, but don't feel limited. Use a separate piece of paper or even a notebook if you need more room.

Why are you doing dōTERRA?

What is the difference you can make in other people's lives by sharing dōTERRA?

How are people better off by having attended one of your classes?

What are some of the benefits of having dōTERRA products in the home?

How can dōTERRA improve the quality of your life?

What do you love to do?

What are you passionate about?

What are your talents and gifts?

YOUR DREAMS

What are 25 things you would do if you had $5,000 more a month?

1. _____
2. _____
3. _____
4. _____
5. _____
6. _____
7. _____
8. _____
9. _____
10. _____
11. _____
12. _____
13. _____
14. _____
15. _____
16. _____
17. _____
18. _____
19. _____
20. _____
21. _____
22. _____
23. _____
24. _____
25. _____

What are three things you could do that would improve the quality of your life?

1. _____

2. _____

3. _____

Write out your ideal day if money or time were not an issue?

What will you have to sacrifice in the short term in order to live your dream in the long term?

1. _____

2. _____

3. _____

4. _____

5. _____

Why will it be worth it?

What do you envision for yourself two years from today? What will you be doing? How will your circumstances have changed?

TO-DOS

☐ Get 40 pictures that inspire you and speak to your heart.

☐ Narrow them down to 20.

☐ Place them on a poster board with enough space to write one word under each picture. Write a word that describes how you feel when you look at each picture.

CHAPTER 4

168 Hours

For everything there is a season,
and a time for every matter under heaven
—Ecclesiastes 3:1

We all have the same amount of time each day, so why do some people get more done than others? STARfish know where their time goes, because time is money—or is it freedom?

Your need for assistance with time management is usually in direct proportion to the distance you are from your calling. The further away you are, the harder it is to stay focused. Many time management experts would have you believe you have a time management problem when in fact your "problem" is only a symptom. The cause is that you are in conflict with your calling.

When you are living your calling, time is much easier to manage. You are drawn by your calling instead of fighting against a job that simply doesn't fit. Granted, we all need to push through tough times and do things we don't feel like doing. However, doing this every day for 40 years is a bit much for anyone.

The average American indulges in around 35 hours of TV and other media per week. Over a 10-year period, that is a total of—get this—18,200 hours!

Not impressed? Let's put it in more meaningful terms. Divided by 40, the number of hours in a typical work week, those 18,200 hours translate into 9.4 *years* of working 40 hours per week at 48 weeks per year.

Did you get that? *Nine-point-four years* parked in front of the TV.

I am not condemning people who watch television. I have my own favorite show, and you will also find me plastered in front of the TV for many college basketball games and *all* of March Madness! But wouldn't you love to have that much time to do something productive?

One of the best ways to discover where your time goes is to complete the 168-Hour Exercise. This exercise will help you to

- Develop your ideal day.
- Identify what you need and want to do.
- Very importantly, identify the time-eaters that are not getting you closer to your dream so you can replace them with activities that will.

This isn't astrophysics. All you do is take each task and figure out how much time you spend on it, first every week, then every year, and then over a 10-year period. Then you assess whether that task is worth your time.

Once you've created your list and completed your assessment, you create a weekly schedule. You should approach it much like you did back when you were in high school. Remember? The bell rang and you went to math. The bell rang again and you went to science. You left science and had lunch, and so on until after school, when you either played sports or went home. At home, you did your homework and chores, ate dinner, and eventually went to bed. (Of course, your schedule might have looked a bit different if you were fortunate enough to be educated at home).

While you might have started your homework in math class, you didn't finish it there. There wasn't time. You went from class to class—and if you were like me, you had your stuff packed up five minutes before the bell rang!

With this example from school days in mind, let's get started organizing your hours in a way that can create a personal pathway toward goals attained and dreams fulfilled.

168-HOUR EXERCISE

Begin by making a list of all the things you have to do each day for an entire week—168 hours—from the time you get up until bedtime. Include things you would love to do but may not be doing currently, such as reading daily inspirational material, working out, playing the piano, or having a date night.

Write down the number of hours you invest in each activity daily. (Since we're talking about 24-hour days, don't forget to include the time you spend sleeping at night). Then add the numbers for every activity together to get its weekly subtotal. Finally, add all those weekly subtotals together to get a grand total of all the hours you've accounted for in your week.

Now subtract that number from 168. How much time do you have left? That number will tell you whether you truly "don't have time"!

Activity	Hours Per Day	Hours Per Week	168

Total Time Remaining:_____

Let's say you wind up with 10 hours left over at the end of the week. Ten hours per week for 48 weeks per year multiplied by 10 years is 4,800 hours. Divide that figure by a 40-hour workweek and you get one hundred twenty 40-hour weeks. That's 2.5 years of 40 hour workweeks to do whatever you choose.

Now ask yourself, "How would my life be different if I spent those 10 hours per week doing what I love, or learning a new skill, or building my business?"

HOW MUCH IS YOUR TIME WORTH?

Ready for the final step? It's time to discover what carelessly misusing your time may be costing you. How much money are you losing? Ultimately, how much freedom? You're about to find out—so you can take steps to upgrade the value of your time to its true worth.

Determine your current or desired hourly income. If you have an annual salary, this table will help you figure out your hourly pay.

My desired or actual annual income: _____

Weekly rate (divide annual income by number of weeks you work per year): _____

Hourly rate (divide weekly rate by number of hours in your workweek): _____

Now multiply your hourly rate by the number of hours you spend in each category on your list. For example, if you'd like to make $26.00 an hour and you watch two hours of TV per night, you are actually spending $52.00 daily on TV, or $260.00 per five-day workweek—and that's not including the cable bill! If you pull over at the local coffee house and spend 30 minutes there, your $4.00 latte costs you $17.00.

Now ask yourself, "Is what I'm doing worth the money I'm spending to do it?"

NOTE: This exercise only applies to activities that are not relational or vital. Don't go figuring out how much it's costing you to have a date night with your spouse and then decide to bail! Relationships are beyond price, and spending time with a loved one is always worthwhile. STARfish understand perfectly the difference between activities that are worth their time versus those that are not.

On the next page, you'll find a list of controllable activities that a STARfish commits to doing every day to guarantee his or her success. STARfish know that a great day starts the night before!

EVENING

- Write out a call list of 30 people for tomorrow
- Write down activity stats
- Refill your supplies
- Record expenses and mileage
- Diffuse two oils for bedtime
- Take supplements
- Review MCM script
- Read goals/vision
- Get seven to eight hours of sleep

MORNING

- Do 20 minutes of inspirational reading
- Review your goals and vision
- Have family breakfast
- Call two people and inspire them
- Review scripts
- Pray

DAYTIME

- Be mentally present all day
- Make at least two new contacts
- Make at least two customer calls
- Make two calls to builders
- Product training
- Attend team call
- Coach builders
- Be coached
- Teach at least one class per week
- Do five or more one-on-ones per week

CHAPTER 5

CONTROLLING THE CONTROLLABLES

I can do all things through him who strengthens me.
—Philippians 4:13

Ask, and it will be given to you: seek, and you will find;
knock, and it will be opened to you. For everyone
who asks receives, and the one who seeks finds,
and to the one who knocks it will be opened.
—Matthew 7:7–11

How do we know what we can control and what we cannot? People often waste valuable energy worrying about things that either never happen or that are out of their direct control instead of finding a way to work with what is right in front of them.

SELLfish tend to focus on things outside of their control—for example, their sales territory. SELLfish say things like, "If I lived in that person's state, I would be crushing it as well," or, "The only reason they have access to all the leaders is because they live in their town."

Or SELLfish let the time of year be their excuse: "People aren't going to do classes in the summer. *Everyone* is on vacation!" "No one does classes during the holidays. They are too busy." How many times have you used such an excuse to get out of doing something that could bring rejection—or even failure? That is often a tough wound to reopen.

STARfish know exactly what they need to do in order to make success 100 percent predictable. By repeating a proven system day after day, they remove the stress from their work. They know that a productive day begins the night before.

They also understand that there are only three things they can control:

1. Their attitude
2. Their work habits
3. How well they serve people

These three areas are what I call *controllables*, and they need no defining. Their meanings are obvious. If only they were as easy to live out as they are to explain! But tucked away inside us are factors that conspire to keep us from controlling the controllables. Things that can block your success if you let them.

But you don't have to let them.

Let's examine how these issues may be affecting you and how you can overcome them. We'll start with one of our most formidable opponents: the three-headed giant known as Fear.

THREE TYPES OF FEAR
FEAR OF REJECTION

Knowing your Why is important. But do you know your Why Not? People are often more paralyzed by their Why Not than they are by the lack of a clear Why.

Give me a person who has learned how to overcome their Why Not over a person with a strong Why any day. When you overcome the Why Nots in life, you'll discover your Why. But people allow excuses to keep them stuck.

The fear of rejection is a huge Why Not. If you don't experience it, then you are not doing network marketing correctly (or any job, for that matter). The point is to not let that fear immobilize you. People are often paralyzed by fear that never materializes. They cannot, for instance, get themselves to pick up the phone or approach a stranger because they are so afraid of what people will think about them. A wise sales manager told me long ago, "Don't worry about what people think about you. They are too busy thinking about themselves."

Fear of rejection reared its ugly head regularly during my door-to-door selling days. I faced it every time I knocked on the next door. But the fear was never justified: the people behind the doors just weren't as scary as I dressed them up to be in my mind. And eventually, I did not feel rejection because I learned how to change my definition of success.

One thing that helped was to separate what I was selling from who I am. I've learned not to take people's "No" personally. Some people will like what I have and others won't. It's not my job to talk them into something they don't want. My job is to make a list and cross people off of it. Some will understand the value of what I'm offering them while others will not. And that's okay.

As long as I focused on seeing a lot of people and left everyone in a better mood than when I found them, it didn't matter to me which ones bought from me. The more people I talked with, the more became customers (funny how that works).

So I tried to collect as many noes as possible and leave every person feeling better for having talked with me. Sales were simply a matter of letting the law of averages work in my favor.

There are buyers on every corner in America. If you took your dōTERRA class bag and started knocking on doors in a nearby neighborhood, the law of averages says that three out of 30 families will enroll. And the law of averages works—I know this beyond doubt from my own long experience in sales.

So don't let the fear of rejection stop you. Instead, change your definition of success. When you learn to reframe every no as just one step closer to the next yes, you can be successful with every invite situation or every class. So what if someone turns you down? You're still engaged in income-producing activity. That's success, is it not? Of course it is. You've narrowed down the odds in your favor, and you're closing in on your next customer. Congratulate yourself—you're right on track!

FEAR OF FAILURE

Does dōTERRA's business model actually work? Can you succeed at selling it? You would not be the first person to ask such questions. The answer to both of them is yes. And your success can be 100 percent predictable when you control the controllables.

There are many successful people involved in dōTERRA who have paved the way for you. They have the same products, the same training, the same compensation plan, and the same business model. What has made the difference? They haven't let fear of failure keep them from their dreams. Instead, they have looked their fear in the eye and said, "Yes I can!" And upon their dreams, they have built magnificent lifestyles. You can too.

FEAR OF SUCCESS

Have you ever known someone who felt it was noble to be poor? Or that to be rich, you have to sell your soul? This is simply faulty programming. Granted, money used or earned by unethical means is wrong. But gaining wealth by ethical means simply means you can do a lot more good in the world.

In our culture, we often attack those with money and assume they acquired it dishonestly. People have been programmed to think it's more honorable to be poor than to have enough money to feed the poor.

Those who live in the paycheck world rarely get the freedom we get. If you really want to change the world, go make a lot of money. Get that part out of the way so you can make it happen!

The following was a Facebook post by our great friend, leader, and dōTERRA Presidential Diamond, Betsy Holmes. She had been traveling to a Rugby Tournament in Bermuda with her husband and business partner, Paul, when they parked across the street from the second largest private yacht in the world. The yacht carried a $475 million price tag and was appointed with two helicopter pads, 24 guest cabins, several hot tubs, swimming pools, and a submarine capable of submerging to 50 meters. Approximately 70 crew members are needed to operate the yacht and serve the guests.

How much poverty could be alleviated with $475 million dollars, Betsy wondered. She wasn't being critical; that's something we're prone to do in the face of extreme indulgence, but for Betsy, the spectacle took her in a different direction. Here is what she said:

> I want to make it clear that I am not judging [the owners]. King
> Solomon was pretty extravagant, and I think that God is extravagant

with us. After all, he created the most beautiful places on earth and beautiful human beings. And I think heaven will top any human-made ocean liner.

Perhaps these billionaires see themselves as giving opportunity and jobs to many people because this boat was made. I don't know, and I don't care. For me, I think that amount of money causes one to dream and takes limitations off of things you never thought possible.

Well, if God owns everything anyway and has much more money than these billionaires, AND you trust him, then that means you are a son or daughter of the richest guy out there, who wants to bless you as his child AND bless you to be a blessing others (also his children). And he doesn't always do that financially because he knows we have more needs than that—needs of the heart.

But, what does it look like for you if $ limitations are taken away? What would you do with $475 million? What is your REAL dream if all limitations were taken away. If it's not to buy a boat, then what is it? Whatever that is—it's your real dream that you maybe didn't think is possible. But that's your real dream! And I think it's possible! That amount of money, at least for most people, takes away thinking about themselves, because no one needs that amount of money just for themselves.

Sure, there are greedy people, and loving money causes all kinds of issues to one's detriment. For me, I know a whole lot of orphans who could use some protection from the world, a safe place to grow up, loving parents, etc. That is the direction I would go with this much $. But I don't view the money so highly or love it—because it takes PEOPLE to change lives, not just money. People who are willing to be the hands and feet of God. People who believe they already have what they need and just get started because they know their dad already has it.

The dream comes before the $ in most cases. Not all dreams even need money. So, like the guy at the end of the movie *Pretty Woman* said, "What's your dream?" Ha ha! This business guy's dream was to build an extravagant boat perhaps. What is yours? Helps me think about this, so I thought it might also help *you* to think on that beautiful dream of yours and stop using $ as the excuse.

So what is your negative programming that you need to change? Do you fear success? Failure? How about rejection?

Our subconscious is frequently in conflict with our conscious mind in ways that can hinder our growth. Unfortunately, the subconscious mind is just that: subconscious, below the surface. So if we want to change our beliefs, we need to change our programming.

PROGRAMMING

In his book *What to Say When You Talk to Yourself,* Dr. Shad Helmstetter discusses how the results we get flow out of what we tell ourselves. Significance and success stems from our actions, which are determined by our feelings, which are based on our attitudes. And our attitudes come from our beliefs, which are simply a matter of programming.

If we buy into our fears, we will have false programming. If we develop the habit of being timid in the face of fear, we will forever remain stuck in life. If excuses appeal to us more than finding a way, we will perpetually have bad programming. And our bad programming will keep us from fulfilling our calling and helping a lot of people along the way.

Let's say you were told at a young age that all rich people are bad. You accept this as truth, and that belief shapes your attitude toward wealthy people. Since you feel negatively toward them, you act in ways that ensure you yourself don't become rich. You may form a victim mentality. You begin to make excuses. You take the easy way out. You want more out of life, but you justify your failure to actively improve your situation, based on your belief that it's okay not to have what you want because being poor is somehow noble.

This mentality keeps us stuck. We tell ourselves, "No one wants to come to a class over the holidays." This affects our self-image, because we know deep down that people *will* come to a class if we ask—and when people do not attend a class, we definitely won't get any enrollments!

So now our confidence level is down. Instead of picking up the phone, we become paralyzed with fear. Fear of what people will say. Fear of getting rejected. Maybe even fear of being successful.

Something has to change. But what—and how?

SELF-TALK

We need to change our programming. And in order to accomplish that, we have to change how we talk to ourselves. We must become aware of our own internal dialogue, assess it, and be careful about what agreements we make with it. For example:

"I'm not good at talking to people."

"People are too busy over the holidays to come to a class."

"Rich people are bad. Having money is the root of all evil!"

These are not good things to tell yourself if you want to run a profitable business! If they've been programmed into your belief system, now is the time to deprogram yourself, because this kind of thinking will keep you stuck. The good news is, you *can* change your thinking by changing the way you talk to yourself.

I was on my way up to New York to teach my first official class. Prior to this, I had done a few one-on-ones and observed many classes, but that was it. I could have excused myself from having high expectations. I could have let my self-talk go something like this: "This is going to be scary! I wonder if anyone will show up—or even enroll. Do I even know enough about the oils yet to teach a class? Maybe I should wait."

Instead, I pictured a full living room. I saw people smiling and digesting the information (and the peppermint brownies). I told myself repeatedly that this was going to be the best class in the history of dōTERRA! I pictured every person filling out the enrollment form and breezing through each information box.

"They are going to love me, and they are going to love the products," I thought. "I'm going to serve them, find out each person's health goals, and then help them accomplish those goals." I told myself that I was coming home with 10 enrollments.

This is how a STARfish talks to himself before a class. And the fruit of my self-talk was a great evening for everyone, with eight enrollments.

So get out there and teach! If you can open a bottle, read the alphabet, and tell your story, and if you understand a little bit about the current state of our healthcare system, you will do fine.

You may feel like you are not ready. You may tell yourself that you will stink. But you *won't* stink, so turn that thought around and tell yourself just the opposite, because that's the truth. You're going to do great. Most people do not know what you know, and your attendees will think you're doing a fabulous job.

ATTITUDE

We have heard about the importance of having a good attitude since the day we first had a bad one. My dad, who was the greatest salesman I've ever met, used to tell me, "Neal, change your attitude." He himself always had the best of attitudes because he always focused on what he could control. He didn't make excuses—he just went to work. It's amazing what that simple, powerful combination of no excuses and hard work can accomplish! Action cures both fear and attitude issues.

Dad used to sell hospital beds for the Hill-Rom Company, which had about 90 percent share in their market. He worked his way up the ladder and ultimately retired as the senior vice-president of sales and service. Not too shabby for a guy who was born at the beginning of the Great Depression. My dad reached his level of success because he had a positive attitude; he always knew that something good would happen if he treated people right and simply went to work.

Showing up is more than half the battle. My dad drove through blizzards in upstate New York, Vermont, and New Hampshire to make calls on hospitals when most people would have made excuses and remained in the comforts of their home office. When he showed up in the middle of a snowstorm, do you think his chance of getting an order increased?

Dad simply refused to let a storm get in his way of helping people. He knew how easy an excuse is to make, but he chose to control how he perceived a situation. That's the attitude of a true STARfish—and attitude is everything.

BELIEF

The Share Success program, developed by the team led by Natalie and Andy Goddard, addresses the vital role that belief plays in our profession. Share Success has done a superb job of mapping out how people's belief level grows as they progress from their initial encounter with dōTERRA to developing a thriving business.

When people first experience the life-changing effects of dōTERRA products, their belief in them begins to increase. The first time I used Deep Blue Rub' on a sore muscle, I realized, *Hey, this stuff works!* Ditto with Breathe to unclog my sinuses. Talk about a confidence builder! Nothing boosts your confidence like knowing your product really is just that good.

As you advance in the business, your belief grows with you: belief in the product, the company, the leaders, the opportunity, and ultimately, in your personal ability to influence others to their benefit and yours. What begins with a foundational belief evolves into a vision beyond what you can see when your dōTERRA products first arrive.

But you don't have to go on some long pilgrimage in order to increase your belief level. Here are six proactive steps you can take that will empower you to take action from the very start, even when you don't know all the ropes.

SIX QUICK STEPS TO BUILDING YOUR BELIEF

1. Focus on why you do what you do and on how it helps people. What if they don't change? What is the impact of their remaining the same?
2. Develop credibility by being a "product of the product." In other words, gain firsthand experience with the products you share by using them yourself and experiencing their benefits.

3. Put in a *ton* of activity. Activity breeds confidence *and* cures fear.
4. Know your intention toward your prospect and how to communicate it quickly.
5. Deliver on your promises.
6. Realize that everyone will be using dōTERRA eventually—and they might as well be on your team!

KNOWLEDGE BREEDS CONFIDENCE

Most of us have heard that "knowledge breeds confidence." The more we know about a subject, the more capable we feel when faced with a situation that requires the knowledge we possess.

I remember the first few times I ran up to a house and knocked on the door. Scary! My sales acumen was formative and my confidence level was low.

But as I learned about human nature, mastered my approach, managed to get all the way through my presentation, and actually began to gain customers, my confidence increased. The same thing will happen for you when people come to one of your classes and end up sharing products with their friends.

CONFIDENCE IN A CLASS

The graph on the next page demonstrates how confidence increases during the course of a class as an attendee gains knowledge.

Let's say you're that attendee. The first time you try dōTERRA, your confidence in the product may be around 5 or 10 percent. (All percentages here are just guesstimates for the purpose of illustration.) Then you go to a class, and your confidence begins to rise as you meet the host and presenter, see other people, and see the products.

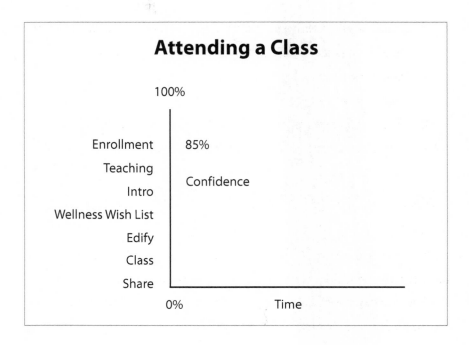

The class starts. The host introduces the speaker, and your confidence level gets another boost as you learn about that person's background, qualifications, and relationship with the host. As you relate to the speaker's story, and as you find yourself agreeing with their interpretation of the current healthcare crisis, your confidence in them and what they are doing rises to 40 percent. You begin to see yourself getting involved in whatever this "party" is about!

Once you start filling out your health goals, you move still further up the confidence scale. By the time you've learned about natural alternatives that can help you meet your goals, you feel about 75 percent confident that you want to get involved.

Now the speaker summarizes what the class has covered, and that reinforces some of the reasons why dōTERRA would be a good fit for you. So you're ready when you hear the invitation, "Would it be okay if I shared with you how to set up your wholesale membership?" You bet! Boom! You enroll.

At this point you are about 85 percent confident in your decision. When will you feel 100 percent confident?

One hundred percent confidence will arrive when you receive your products and have a few positive experiences with them. This is when a wellness consultation can make or break your reaching 100 percent.

Hint: Don't wait to schedule a wellness consultation. Do so at the class.

CONFIDENCE IN SHARING

Remember the night when you enrolled? Take a minute. What was it like signing the enrollment form? Leaving the host's house? Walking through your own front door and explaining to your spouse what you had just gotten yourself into?

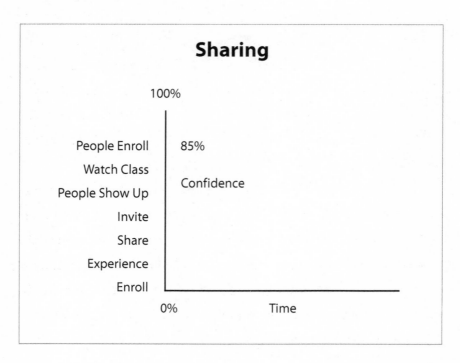

If your spouse had inquired then about your desire to build a business, you might have replied that you had zero interest. But was it really your interest that was lacking—or your confidence that you could do it? With each new experience with dōTERRA, you likely became more interested and more confident in your abilities.

From the time you get your first products, your dōTERRA sharing journey follows a predictable path. As you experience the powerful effects of the products, you begin to tell your friends. Much as you'd do with a good movie or restaurant, you can't help but share with those who you feel could benefit from the same experience you've had. So share you do, and your confidence increases. You invite a few friends to a class, and they actually show up! Then as you watch your sponsor teach the class, your confidence rises and you think, "Hey, I can do that!"

At the end of the class, you feel excited. A few of your friends are actually enrolling! You're now about 85 percent confident that you've got what it takes to conduct a class yourself and even build a little team.

When will you be 100 percent confident? When you do a class and enroll your first person. This is why, if you are leading a team, it's critical to get your team members to each teach their own class and enroll their first person as soon as possible. Doing so will have a massive effect on their confidence as well as their ability to duplicate quickly.

Don't wait on the sidelines, hoping someone will knock on your door or private-message you with a request to enroll. Those situations may occur, but you can't count on them, and a passive approach will get you nowhere. You need to be active, and so do the team members you enroll. Guide them to the point where they can teach and enroll people on their own. Because the ability to enroll others is what can change lives—including yours!

TWO TYPES OF PEOPLE

There are only two types of people in the world. One looks for a way; the other looks for an excuse. Guess which one is the STARfish and which one is the SELLfish.

It's human nature to cop out. Most people are experts not only at excuse creation but also at strategic execution. Finding an excuse is easy; finding a way is not.

We all face difficult situations at times. That is life. We may not always be completely responsible for what happens to us, but we are 100 percent responsible for how we respond. And how you respond is what will make all the difference. Will you find an excuse, or will you find a way?

During college and law school, I worked for the oldest direct-selling company in the United States, selling educational books and software door-to-door. Every summer when college was out, I used to attend the company's week-long, intensive sales and leadership school along with a host of other students from all over the United States. Once the school was over, we all went our separate ways to different parts of the country, found our own places to live, got up at 5:59 every morning, took an ice-cold shower, and then went door-to-door for 14 hours, six days a week, working on straight commission and paying all of our own expenses. There were no guarantees except that we would hear "No" a lot! One summer I worked hard enough to finish in the top 30 out of over 3,000 students.

That same year in the fall, I returned to Indiana University needing 45 credit hours to graduate. In order to begin law school the following year, as I had decided to do, I would have to take 23 credit hours one semester and 22 the next. Considering that full-time is 12 to 15 credit hours, taking on so much coursework was a daunting proposition. And I was already spearheading a student sales group at IU for my company! So extra time was not something I felt I had.

But I wasn't going to let those concerns stop me. I knew I could find a way because I had developed the habit of doing so. I completed the necessary credits, graduated a semester early, and accomplished my goal of entering law school the following fall.

Throughout my six years selling books door-to-door, I wanted to quit countless times. Fortunately, I had learned the STARfish's secret of controlling my three controllables: my attitude, my work habits, and how well I served people.

Too often we fail to take responsibility not only for our actions but also our inaction. But the short-term comfort of making excuses catches up with us in the long run. Eventually we have to take responsibility for how we will react to life's challenges.

My personal decision to act and never quit has not only changed my life but also served as an example that helps hundreds of others believe they too can push a little harder, knock on one more door, and take the yeses and noes in stride. The yeses pay the bills, but the noes build character, so don't let them discourage you. Wanting to quit is okay. Quitting is not.

We need to be people who find a way when it looks like we have no options. This country needs us. Our community needs us. Our family needs us to be the best we can be. There is always a way.

You can be a light. You can provide hope. You can provide inspiration and healing to so many people right in your community and around the world. People are hurting, and if we quit, if we fail to find a way, then others suffer.

Much of the joy that comes in this life is having an attitude of gratitude and being that person who finds a way over, under, and around any obstacle. As Chris Brady from Life Leadership says, "There is no safety in a significant life and no significance in a safe life."

WORK HABITS

STARfish concentrate on their work habits and activity, not their results. They control how hard and how smart they work, and they purposefully choose the activities on which they will focus.

Conversely, SELLfish focus on results, recognition, and what people think of them. Scrambling to achieve a higher rank, they sidestep honest effort and patience in favor of shortcuts. They sell on Amazon or blast the Internet and poach other people's prospects because they are too lazy to find their own.

STARfish know there are no shortcuts. Period. They know that the best way to get results is to break down the end result (an enrollment) into little activities that lead to enrollment.

Those smaller activities are so important! That's why STARfish keep a log of how many contacts they've made, shares they've done, invites they've given, classes they've held, and many other significance-producing activities. (You'll find a list coming up shortly.)

When you know your numbers, you take the pressure off yourself, and then sharing is fun! STARfish find their self-esteem in work habits, not production. Production is simply the fruit of proper work habits.

"How many contacts does it take you to get someone to enroll?" It's a question I often ask, and usually the other person hasn't a clue.

"What is your enrollment percentage?" Crickets.

"What is your enrollment to LRP percentage?" "What is your PV per class?" Crickets times two.

Finally, "What rank would you like to achieve in the next 60 days?" Maybe the person isn't sure, but often they'll say, "I'd like to be Gold."

"Do you know how many contacts and classes you need in order to achieve that rank?" Usually crickets again.

A STARfish doesn't do crickets. Knowing your ratios allows you to predict the activity you need to perform in order to get the result you desire. Otherwise—ever begin a month not knowing how many classes you need to teach? That is pressure!

If your average PV per class is 1,000 and you need 3,000 in volume, then you will need to do three classes (minus LRP) to hit your goal! So at the beginning of the month you can look at how many classes you have set and know within a few hundred PV what your volume will be or how many classes you still need to fill. Knowing up front what action you need to take will let you breathe a lot easier than getting to the end of the month and freaking out.

The following list will help you keep track of your numbers and plan the smaller activities that lead to big results.

SIGNIFICANCE-PRODUCING ACTIVITIES
- Calls
- Shares
- Samples given
- Invites
- Classes scheduled
- Classes held

- Invites who attended
- Invites who enrollled
- Invites who did LRP
- New classes set from the class
- Referrals
- Wellness consults set
- Wellness consults performed

THE LAW OF AVERAGES

Why wait to get started. Why think about whom you are going to call. Just pick up the phone and make the call. Let's say you have three people on your list, and you make the calls, and no one accepts an invitation to your class. What do you do? Quit? Never. You learn to fall in love with the law of averages.

When you focus on performing an activity, you will discover that good things often happen long after a focus on production would have told you to quit. For example . . .

Imagine a neighborhood with 15 houses on each side of the street. Based on the law of averages, there are likely three enrollments in those 30 houses. All you have to do is knock. (Yes, I know, we don't share our products door-to-door—at least, not yet! But you get the picture.)

Most people knock on the first few doors, get three noes, and stop. "It doesn't work." "No one wants to buy." "I'm bothering people. I wonder what they will think about me."

Others drive to a coffee shop to *think* about making more calls. Or they listen to one more positive CD or browse a few pages from *The Greatest Salesman in the World* for an attitude boost. What they don't do is keep knocking.

But you're game to try a couple more doors. So what happens when you get to the fifth house and no one has enrolled? Do you keep going and play the law of averages? Or do you go home and wait until you *feel* like making more calls?

Using our example above, perhaps you've already discovered in your business that three enrollments are usually found in the last eight houses. So if you stop when you feel like stopping rather than at a time you've predetermined, you'll never be able to help those last three people who would enroll if you simply showed up.

As you keep going, you gain momentum. Your names start to roll. You gain confidence. And God rewards your perseverance. But you have to be out there.

So embrace the beginning stages of your business. People who want to be an expert right out of the gate end up doing nothing. Their pride is more important than their dreams. Some won't teach a class because they feel they need to know the entire Modern Essentials book word for word. Others wait for inspiration to hit before they make the call or set the class, not realizing that activity is what breeds passion. This is why so many people are paralyzed by fear. They procrastinate doing the activity that scares them the most, and all it does is turn into a monster that devours their dreams.

Never quit knocking. Never give up on a day, a week, or a month. Good things happen after five o'clock on Friday. Good things happen the last few days of the month. Good things are going to happen behind the next door down. All you have to do is knock.

SERVING PEOPLE

When your mind is on service, you're never nervous. STARfish have a clear picture of what they want to accomplish and whom they can help. They know that action cures all fear and that action or inaction is what determines our feelings.

If you want to feel a certain way, you need to act a certain way. You don't need to read another page in your self-help book, learn another oil, or wait another 15 minutes before you pick up the phone. You will never feel like doing something more than at the moment when you know you should be doing it.

When you focus on serving people, you take the focus off of yourself and put it on them. If you are nervous approaching someone or picking up the phone, it is probably because you're thinking about what *you* want instead of what the customer wants. Concentrate instead on how our product will help them.

Having systems in place, knowing what you're going to say, and focusing on simply doing the next activity, whether it's a contact, a share, a class, or an enrollment—these are part of the way you think when you're a STARfish.

The SELLfish, on the other hand, focuses on getting the sale and getting out of there before the customer changes her mind. Since SELLfish rarely follow up, they get few referrals. And because they make so few contacts each day, naturally they feel nervous approaching people— because every contact has got to count. They don't let the law of averages play to their favor. When you commit to making 10 or more contacts per day, then you know that a few of them will want to come to a class. But if you are only making one or two, you need every person to attend. That's good old-fashioned sales pressure on you and on your customer.

The STARfish cares about making a difference at every house and with every person, regardless of whether anyone enrolls. When your goal is to deliver value, not make a sale, then the pressure is off of everyone.

Before I teach a class, I picture myself leaving every person in a better mood than when they arrived. I want their son or daughter to tell their parents, "Wow, that was a really cool person! He was different. I want to be like him." I want parents telling each other how they admire the way I do the job—how I work hard and treat people well regardless of whether they enroll.

I picture people learning about attitude by seeing how positive mine is when someone tells me no. I want my impact on a family to go far beyond oils and products. When I leave their house after 10:00 P.M., I want the bounce in my step to renew their hope in direct selling and in people in general.

I picture some kid working harder for her dreams because she noticed me working hard for mine. Helping her achieve significance in the future is the Why that drives me.

I know that I can be successful when I redefine what success means to me. It's not about enrollments. When your goal is selling and you fail to sell, you are down. But when you focus on controlling what you can control—your attitude, your work habits, and your commitment to serve people for their own sake regardless of the outcome—then success is yours.

Every time.

CHAPTER 6

How People Buy

People don't buy what you are selling;
they buy what you get them to say.
—Neal Anderson

S TARfish know how people buy and have mastered the process customers go through before they make a buying decision. STARfish know what people like and what they don't like, and as a result, they have cultivated four qualities that SELLfish don't possess.

1. STARFISH KNOW THAT PEOPLE LOVE TO BUY BUT DISLIKE BEING SOLD

Have you ever listened to a sales pitch in which the salesperson did 99 percent of the talking? They were so excited to show you their new widget (or oils) that they totally forgot the most important factor in sharing successfully: YOU!

One day, while I was filling up our Jeep with gas, a guy in a black Suburban pulled up next to me and asked, "Hey, I have an extra home entertainment system. Do you want one?" (Yes, I know—a little strange, but not to a former door-to-door salesman). I replied, "No thank you."

He responded enthusiastically with the old "I can give you a really good deal on it." I politely said no. His determination to find a way to sell his last system of the day at a gas pump was commendable, but he did not understand how people buy. He was sort of a SELLfish.

A STARfish knows that he needs to make it all about the other person, and he seeks to put that person at ease. He builds a sharing environment by reassuring the prospect that it's okay to say no if the product isn't for him. Because the STARfish prioritizes the prospect's well-being, he will leave that person in a good mood regardless of his buying decision.

The STARfish will also ask a lot of questions before talking about the product. Had my salesman in the Suburban been a STARfish, he would have said, "Hey sir, I know this may sound kind of crazy, but I'm the one who has been sitting down with a lot of families here in the North Raleigh area and installing these really cool home entertainment systems. I know you may not be in the market for one, but if you watch a fair amount of TV or movies and would like to get a really good value on a system, would it be worth taking a few minutes to at least check it out? I promise to leave you in a good mood either way."

2. STARFISH ARE IN A HURRY!

Don't you hate it when a salesperson promises it'll "only take a minute" for you to hear their pitch, and then they end up taking an hour! SELLfish rarely ask, "Is this is a good time?" or "I didn't catch you in the middle of something important, did I?" They go right into their pitch regardless of your time or interest.

Not a STARfish. She acknowledges that most people are busy, so she has a sense of urgency, and she lets people know right away. She apologizes for being in a hurry and is honest when she says it will only take a few minutes. This approach increases trust, and it allows her to get to the point quickly and invite people to learn more about her products.

So before someone tells you they don't have time, get there first. Let them know that you regret being so hasty, but you only have a quick minute. And mean it!

3. STARFISH ARE NOT PUSHY

The third reason people dislike SELLfish is because they are pushy. No one likes dealing with a salesperson who pressures them to do something they do not want to do.

I once listened to an audio recording of a conversation between a service representative for a major cable company and a customer who called to cancel his account. The rep would not comply with the gentleman's request. Instead he went on and on, putting pressure on the caller, trying to talk the man out of his express wishes.

Have you ever had the delight of receiving a call during dinner from a telemarketer who tried to keep you on the phone even though you told him you were in the middle of supper with your family? Or walked into a store and found yourself almost instantly telling a little white lie? You know: the first thing the clerk said to you was, "Can I help you?" And you replied, "No, I'm *just looking.*" You experienced pressure, even though the clerk felt she was just helping you.

You do like to buy, though, don't you? Sure you do. Under the right circumstances and given a product you truly desire, it's a pleasure to spend your money on something you know you'll be happy with.

By creating a safe, unpressured sales environment, STARfish help their customers enjoy the process of purchasing products whose value to them is clear and which they know they'll be glad they bought. Buying is fun when you can relax, get helpful information, and freely choose to purchase for the right reasons.

4. STARFISH LEAVE PEOPLE IN A GREAT MOOD

SELLfish are so focused on making the sale that they may unintentionally leave people in a bad mood when the customer says no. They tend to argue with prospects and say things like, "Don't you want to be healthy?" Or they may leave the class exasperated because people didn't enroll.

That's not how STARfish operate. They put the interests of others first, and their customers can tell.

When people know that you genuinely care about what's best for them, to the extent that you can graciously take no for an answer, they will appreciate your attitude—and you. You can be someone who makes their day a little better. That's the mark of a STARfish. And remember, what goes around comes around. Sow a blessing and reap its fruit.

CREATING A SHARING ENVIRONMENT

How does it feel to deal with a salesperson who instantly puts pressure on you? Think about it for a few seconds. What are some of the things you are thinking? Feeling? Are you excited to be in this conversation? Of course not!

STARfish take the pressure off at the very beginning of any customer interaction, whether it is face-to-face, a phone call, a Facebook or text message, or a conversation at the beginning of a class. They create a sharing environment by letting people know right away that if they like what they see, great, but if not, that is totally okay. STARfish will leave their prospects in a great mood regardless of whether they decide to move forward.

Remember, there is an elephant in the room before any selling situation takes place. The elephant is people's fear barrier. They are thinking, "Will I have to buy anything, and if I don't, will I get out of here alive?" You can help them move past their apprehension by creating a sharing environment. That is likely the number one thing STARfish do to set themselves apart from other salespeople. You can have the highest rank or years of business experience, but if you don't know how to create a sharing environment, then you will likely hear a lot of noes.

You need to give people permission to say no so they will feel comfortable saying yes. The sharing atmosphere takes away most of the pressure. When you contact people or invite them to a class, remember that your main goal is serving people and helping them get what they want.

Here is an example of what I will say at the beginning of a class to address the Fear Elephant:

> I appreciate everyone's coming tonight. Before we get started, I have a few rules.
>
> First, tonight is going to be entirely about you and helping you learn about some tools and ideas that can help you gain access to safer, cheaper, and more effective healthcare options.
>
> The second rule is this: How many of you have ever been to a home party—you know, where everyone gets together and you hear about a product and then you end up going home with your twelfth spatula or another handbag (no disrespect, 31 folks)? Well,

tonight we are going to teach you some things that will change your life and if you decide that dōTERRA is a fit for you and your family, then that is great. We will get you set up tonight and you will be on your way to living the dōTERRA lifestyle in a few days.

But if you decide that it's not for you, then it is totally okay to tell me no. One of the things I dislike is being pressured into buying something or feeling like I have to get something simply because I came to a party or presentation. No one likes that.

We are simply passionate about helping people who see dōTERRA as a fit. And as for those who don't, you will be left in a better mood than when you came, and you will leave with a great education. Does that sound okay? Excellent!

PSYCHOLOGICAL PATH OF THE BUYING PROCESS

STARfish know how to guide people through the buying process, which includes both educating them and motivating them. People do not usually embrace what is best for them without a little education and motivation.

As Terry Weaver writes in his book *The Secrets of Selling from the Masters*, "All buyers must take a mental and emotional journey down that buying path. Everyone receives input from both the right and left sides of the brain. Consequently, your presentation must address both sides to be successful. Your two primary functions are *educating* and *motivating* your prospect."

Often we do too much educating. We talk about facts and features instead of benefits. We speak to the head instead of the heart. Speaking to the head causes people to think, and that's good, but speaking to the heart causes them to feel—and it's the feeling part that causes people to buy.

Have you ever had someone tell you they "want to think about it"? As Terry describes, thinking causes procrastination while feeling results in action. We need to balance how we share information so we don't do too much educating and not enough motivating.

THE BUYING LINE

STARfish know when people are ready to make a buying decision. They also know that there is a process people must go through in order to be emotionally *and* logically invested in the offer.

So STARfish do not skip steps, and they do not get off-script. They use a duplicable system to ensure that each person gets the information they need in the most efficient way that allows them to make a decision.

Every product, service, or idea has a *buying line* as well as a best path for guiding people along that buying line and helping them make the best decision in the least amount of time with the least amount of frustration.

The chart on the following page illustrates how the buying line works. Let's apply it to a class. As the class progresses, interest goes up. The key is to know when people have enough interest to make a decision, and to not waste time once they've reached that point. We do this by asking questions throughout the course of the class (or the phone call, or the one-on-one).

There is another buying line for getting people to a class, but you can miss its buying zone if you take too much time talking about the products instead of inviting the person to a class. Talk too much and people are likely to become disinterested.

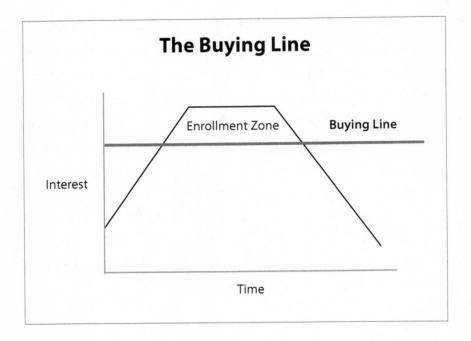

The adult attention span is between eight seconds and 40 minutes. The average attention span of a goldfish is nine seconds! So closing the class should begin at about the 43-minute mark. Unfortunately, SELLfish often talk way past the point at which people are ready to buy. Some people are ready to enroll before the class begins! Others are ready halfway through the class, still others at the end, and some are never ready—and that's okay.

When I help people begin to sell a product, service, or idea, I help them focus on what they need to ask, say, and do to help people get to the buying line in the most efficient manner. Often a SELLfish will talk and talk and talk about their product when the customer is already in the buying zone. "I just need to show her one more oil to get her to buy," the wellness advocate is telling herself—but the customer is ready to purchase *now*! Ultimately the sale is lost because the buyer becomes frustrated. And we all know that a frustrated buyer does not buy.

STARfish understand that people don't necessarily buy products—
they buy ideas that will solve their problems. Perhaps you've heard the
story about the guy who walks into a hardware store and asks the clerk
to recommend a good drill. The clerk goes on and on about all the
features of every drill in the store. Finally, after about 15 minutes, the
man gets frustrated. "Son, I appreciate your taking the time to explain
each of these drills," he says to the clerk, "but I didn't come here today
because I want to buy a drill. I want a hole!"

How many times do we make our presentation all about our
product and fail to help people find the "hole" they are really looking
for—better health, improved mental performance, less anxiety, and
other benefits that dōTERRA products can provide.

THE SHARE CYCLE™

A disciple is not above his teacher, but everyone when he is fully trained will be like his teacher.

—Luke 6:40

Have you wondered if there is a better way to help people through the process they go through from knowing little about dōTERRA all the way through enrolling? Do you struggle to get your team up to speed quickly? Have you ever reached the end of a class and heard the old "Let me talk to my husband" or "Let me think about it"?

Chapter 7 addresses these and other concerns by taking you through the Share Cycle™. This is easily the longest chapter in the book, with insights that can make a dramatic difference in your dōTERRA journey.

The Share Cycle is a system that provides a common language to describe the process through which people go from having never heard about dōTERRA to enrolling and providing you with referrals. When you can break down the process into individual steps and then, over time, master each step, you drastically increase your enrollment percentage and ultimately duplicate more quickly.

We'll cover some of the steps quickly. Others, we'll spend time covering in-depth. Each of them is vital to your success.

FOUR KEYS TO GETTING A DECISION

Before we get into the Share Cycle, we need to discuss the big picture it fits into. There are four questions a STARfish knows the answer to by the time she concludes a customer interaction. Those answers will optimize your chances of getting enrollments. So as you read each step of the Share Cycle, keep the following in mind:

1. Do you know the pain?
2. Do they have money?
3. What is the decision making process?
4. What is the next step?

PAIN

People do not buy features and benefits, as many in sales are taught. *They buy avoidance of pain and/or a move towards pleasure.* But we often miss that point when we talk too much about the products. Is there any dissatisfaction going on in the life of your potential customer? Find out!

MONEY

You've reached the end of teaching a class, and now you hear it: "I don't have the money" or "That's a lot of money!" Frustrating, isn't it. But often it's just an excuse people use to avoid making a decision. After all, most people purchase plenty of things that either are not in their budget or are "too expensive." Consider the average house, car, and toys that may be gathering dust in the garage. We have all purchased things that were "not in our budget" or that we didn't really need.

Of course, it's possible that a person truly is not in a financial position to make a buying decision. So don't get so excited about your product that you fail to qualify your prospect. Does he or she in fact have the money necessary to make the purchase?

Usually, though, the real question is, Are they willing to spend their money on what you are sharing?

You can begin to address that concern before a class gets underway, because it is important to put people at ease regarding any issues with money. One way to do so is to mention that what they are going to see tonight is something everyone can afford. There is something for everyone. And in light of health and wellness being so important here in (name of town/city), people are investing in things that can help improve health, decrease costs, and support the family's overall well-being.

Knowing the budget people have to work with is a key to taking the pressure off your prospects. More times than not, when someone says, "It's not in the budget," they don't even have a budget—and if they do, you can probably create a wellness category in it provided you can demonstrate the need for one.

If something is important enough to someone, they will find the money. Think about this: The Natural Solutions kit is around $550. A person may tell you he doesn't have that kind of money. But what would happen if someone offered him a brand new Jeep Wrangler on sale for $550? Would he find the money? When people tell you they don't have money, they usually do. You just haven't convinced them that your product is worth the price.

DECISION MAKING PROCESS

dōTERRA sounds great, an attendee tells you, but she needs to talk to her husband, or she wants to think about it.

One way to avoid this objection is to discover who makes the decision (which is usually the mom in dōTERRA) and how that person typically goes about making purchasing decisions. Some people can decide on the spot. Others have to have a family board meeting before spending anything over 25 dollars!

NEXT STEP

"I'll get back to you." "Let me think it over." "The class sounds interesting. Call me again after the holidays."

People's responses suggest actions you need to take. Do you always have a next step on the calendar? When you enroll people, do you schedule a wellness consult before they leave the class?

By asking yourself, "What is the next step?" you will discover up front whether people are simply too nice to say no or are truly interested. Sometimes the next step is the last step because they are not interested. And that is fine.

THE SHARE CYCLE™

We'll begin our discussion of the Share Cycle™ itself by getting an overview. The chart on the next page gives you a graphic illustration of the order of the cycle.

Beginning with "Fish" and proceeding clockwise, you progress through 10 key steps, concluding with "Referrals/Follow-up." In actual practice, since you're normally working with a number of

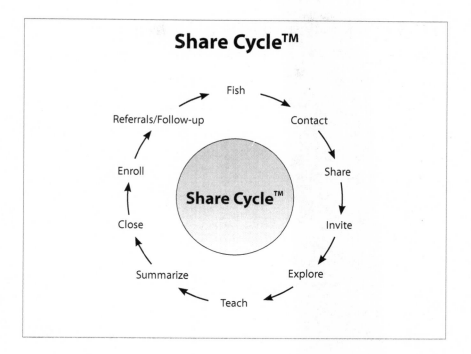

people at the same time, you may find yourself running multiple share cycles and dealing with a different step in each of those cycles. Regardless, the order of steps for every person is always the same. However, some people may spend less time than others in one step or another. Let's take a closer look at each of those steps.

STEP 1: FISH

Fishing is simply finding the ideal customer for what you have. The key is to have as many poles in the water as possible so you can have an endless supply of new people to help.

Fortunately for our business, pretty much everyone is a prospect. However, the ideal customer is someone who falls into one the following three categories:

1. They are already into natural alternatives.
2. They do not like the side effects of a prescription, or they don't like what their doctor is recommending.
3. They are dealing with changes in healthcare. Perhaps their copay has increased, or their insurance has a high deductible, or their doctor is no longer in the network. In any case, they want to create their first line of defense at home.

The first part of fishing is to develop a list of people with whom you can share. The larger your list, the less pressure you will feel. It's amazing how many people come out of the woodwork when you go through Facebook friends, LinkedIn, church directories, neighbors, friends, and family. Networking groups are another way to increase exposure, but be careful that you do not attend just to sell your stuff! Networking is about building relationships, and those take time.

Sharing dōTERRA online is a hot topic that we will save for another day. However, you should know this much: Before you share online, you have got to get your arms around the principles and systems contained in this book. Otherwise, your future success online will be greatly diminished and you'll risk gaining a SELLfish reputation.

The second part of fishing is to find out everything you can about the person you plan to call. By familiarizing yourself with your prospects before you call them, you'll build trust more quickly.

LinkedIn is a great way not only to fish but also to learn critical information about people so you can find a common bond. For example, before you call a chiropractor, look her up in LinkedIn and see which of your connections might know her. You can then call that person and ask them to tell you a little bit about the chiropractor. Often your connection will call the chiropractor or write an email connecting the two of you. LinkedIn is an unlimited list of leads and intelligence, and Facebook can be beneficial as well.

STEP 2: CONTACT

Your success and significance in life will be in direct proportion to the number of times you put yourself and others in a position to say yes or no.

There are only four possible results when you contact someone.

You may get a yes.

You may get a no.

You may get a no with a life lesson.

Or you may be met with procrastination.

Any of these results in itself is no big deal. So why is it such an issue for us to pick up the phone and invite a friend to a class? What goes through our heads just before we do? Are we excited—or hoping they don't answer our call? I know how it goes. I've been there.

To be successful, we need to take the emotion out of making the contact. The worst that can happen is that someone says no.

Yes is a great answer. But no is a great answer too. And no with a life lesson is a great answer. Only procrastination can sap the life out of us. It leaves us with a false hope that the person will come to a class or enroll or call us back when they ask for our card. But in reality, procrastination is often just a way people disguise their "No" because they're too nice to refuse us directly.

So how do you handle procrastination? Proactively. If a person asks you for your card, ask for theirs in return; then in a few days, if they haven't called you, you call them. If someone says they want to think about it, have a follow-up plan. Don't leave a loose end untied if you can help it. Figure out how to give the person a second chance to say either yes or no.

FOUR STAGES OF INTEREST

We often feel pressure in the contacting phase because we focus on the end result instead of the next step. We do the other person no good by mentally jumping them ahead of where they're actually at. So it's essential to recognize the four stages of interest people move through when they become wellness advocates.

First is the *learning stage*. This is where people come to a class or a one-on-one meeting, or perhaps they attend an online webinar. From there, they proceed to the *living stage*, where they become a "product of the product" by experimenting with the various products and gaining firsthand knowledge.

When someone gains sufficient experience with the products, they're ready to leave their comfort zone and move on to the *sharing stage*. Much like when they have a good experience at a restaurant or see a good movie and can't wait to tell others about it, people who use dōTERRA want to share the benefits with those around them.

Finally, fourth comes the *building stage*, in which people are actively growing their business, training their builders, and attempting to supplement or replace their income.

The pressure people often feel when they're fishing comes from trying to put people in stage two, three, or four too quickly. This is one of the main reasons why so many people are averse to network marketers.

Most of the companies in our profession lead with the opportunity. You know—they call you up and tell you about this great new chance to live the dream or make a lot of money. Not only is this approach unprofessional but it ignores the natural progression people go through when building belief in a product or cause. (See the discussion on belief in chapter 5.)

People naturally want to first learn something about the products and the company, and then have a chance to experience the products, before committing to build a new business.

It's foolish to attempt selling the dream before the person trusts the dreamer, yet it still happens every day. And every day another person becomes disenchanted with network marketing. Every day another saleswoman feels scared to pick up the phone because she's supposed to talk her prospect into doing something he knows zero about.

Thankfully, we in dōTERRA have a much better way: understanding how to serve people where they are instead of luring them prematurely down a glowing path with promises of fancy cars and the dream lifestyle. Those things will come—but only after they put in the hard work.

COMMUNICATION 101

Perhaps you've heard that communication is 7 percent word; 38 percent tone, rate, and volume; and 55 percent body language

Most people will evaluate the emotional aspects of your message not by the words you use but by your nonverbal cues and signals. So it is critical that you do a few things to ensure you communicate the right message.

First, slow down and speak in a low voice. It's easy to get nervous when you contact someone. You know the feeling: your voice rises in pitch and you speak faster than you usually do. Have you ever experienced a nervous telemarketer? He didn't sound normal, did he? He spoke so fast that you couldn't understand him—because he knew that if he kept talking, you couldn't interrupt him with an "I'm not interested." Don't you be that way. Just monitor your speaking voice, that's all.

Also, watch your body language. Are you moving back and forth? Are your body actions inconsistent with our words? Do you wave your hands around, shift your eyes, or change positions often? These behaviors all convey nervousness, not confidence.

Remember, people are *feeling* what you are saying more than they are paying attention to your actual words. They get distracted by out-of-sync body gestures, lack of eye contact, and too many filler words such as "um" and "you know."

Finally, keep in mind that people think seven times faster than you talk. You can be in the middle of mentioning the benefits of Peppermint while standing in a grocery line, and your prospect is already thinking, "I like this. It sounds pretty cool! How do I get it?" So be sensitive to where they're at. Don't go on and on about the oils and fail to invite the person to come to your next class!

FIVE WAYS TO CONTACT PEOPLE

There are five ways you can contact people:

1. Face-to-face
2. Phone
3. Text/instant message
4. Invitation
5. Facebook/social media post

The best way to contact someone is of course face-to-face. It's a lot more difficult to tell someone no to his or her face. In fact, it is often harder for a prospect to say no than for a wellness advocate to hear it!

When we make a contact, we want to make sure we have completed the Fish stage so we have information about the person that we can use. And we will want to remember why people don't like salespersons: They are pushy. They leave people in a bad mood. They take up too much time. And they fail to understand people's needs.

We want to create a sense of urgency by apologizing up front to those we contact for being in a big hurry. We're sorry—we only have a quick second. This lets people know that our interaction won't take all day.

Here's how an initial phone contact might go:

Hi Sally, this is Betty. I apologize for being in such a big hurry. Let me quickly tell you what I'm doing.

Do you know how healthcare costs are rising—I mean with copays and high deductibles? And a lot of people don't want to take prescription drugs these days? Well I have been teaching classes right here in the Raleigh area (or around the country) on how to use natural alternatives to support your health.

Have you ever heard about using essential oils and other natural products as an alternative to traditional healthcare? I've been teaching these classes in which people are now using essential oils and other natural products that everyone has been super-excited about. I want to invite you to one of my upcoming classes.

Have you ever used natural medicines? Are you open to learning how to take care of your family naturally? Great, I'm having a class next Tuesday at 7:00 P.M. and another one next Thursday at 6:30. Based on your situation, I feel you would love to learn more. Which one of those dates would work best for you?

People often will not fully hear or comprehend what you say. So be prepared to go back over it again. Remember, people think seven times faster than you talk. You might say,

> I apologize. I guess you haven't had a chance to hear about what I've been doing here in Raleigh? No problem. Like I said, my name is —

and then go right back into the initial conversation.

Some key phrase are meant to engage people. For instance: "Do you know how healthcare is getting expensive?" Here's a sample one-on-one script:

> Do you know how people go to the doctor, and the doctor ends up writing a prescription that creates side effects—and people either can't handle the side effects or they simply don't want to take the medication?
>
> Well, I help people use natural products to help support their overall health and wellness. For example, last week I was working with Sally Smith, and she was congested. I was able to get her a sample of the Respiratory Blend (have the person smell it), and it helped support her breathing.
>
> Just the other day, my son threw up. We didn't want to go to the doctor, so we were able to use this awesome Protective Blend. We put a few drops on the bottoms of his feet, and he didn't throw up again the entire evening and never experienced the all-out flu.

It is important to know exactly how many people you are going to call and whom you are going to call before you start making contacts. One of the best success principles in this area is to have a list of 20 to 30 names sitting on your desk before you start making the calls. We all know how hard it is to make calls when we're flying by the seat of our pants.

Your job is not to sell people. Your job is to make a list and then cross people off it one by one. Some people will want to come to a class; some will not. Some people will procrastinate accepting the invite, and others will say they are going to come but never show up. So memorize this little saying and rehearse it in your head:

Some will. Some won't. So what! Who's next?

Again, your job is simply to make a list and then cross people off it. You need contacts, classes, and enrollments to have a good week. Who's next . . . and next . . . and next . . . ?

ANSWER A QUESTION WITH A QUESTION

The person you're talking with has just asked you The Question: "What do you do?" What do you tell her?

A million ideas flood your head—too many. What was that clever line a colleague used? You can't remember; your brain is frozen. You could just say, "I sell essential oils"—but what if the person is allergic to the scent? Then you've ruined an opportunity. It wouldn't be the first time that has happened.

Remember this timeless principle: Answer a question with a question. First, learn why the person is asking. Usually there is a reason, and once you discover it, you can customize your answer to fit your prospect's situation. That approach has far more potential than simply answering the person's question directly and getting an unpleasant surprise. That's how to lose a perfectly good customer.

Back in my real estate days, I heard a story about a husband and wife who were looking for vacation property in South Carolina. The wife asked whether the community had a golf course. The salesman replied enthusiastically that it did—and promptly discovered that a golf course isn't always a selling point. The wife didn't want to live in a community with a golf course because she would never see her husband!

A STARfish would have told the wife that it was a great question and then inquired why she asked. Once the wife informed him about her husband's golf habit, the salesperson could have asked her other questions to discover her interests. He might have found that she would enjoy a day at the spa or fellowship with the other ladies at the club while her husband played golf. Or he could have explained to her that ownership in a community with a golf course would be a major benefit for increasing the property value, as many people seek a community with a golf course, especially in Hilton Head, South Carolina.

You should always answer the question "What do you do?" with a question, especially at networking events. For instance:

> It really depends. Sometimes I'm changing diapers, and other times I'm playing referee; sometimes I'm fixing boo-boos, and other times I'm traveling. By the way—what do *you* do?

Get them talking about themselves first. Ask great questions, and then they will become genuinely interested in what you do. Then you can begin asking other questions.

> Do you know how a ton of people these days are looking for natural alternatives to traditional healthcare? You know—because most insurance is expensive to buy and more expensive to use, and then you have all those prescriptions and things in a medicine cabinet that have all those harmful side effects. I was talking with one person the other day, and she couldn't believe some of those things are still legal to sell!
>
> So, what I do is work with doctors, nurses, chiropractors, professional athletes, families, and folks just like us, and I teach them

how to use natural alternatives that end up being safer, cheaper, and more effective forms of healthcare. Are you like most people and into that type of stuff? Why is it so important to you? Everyone seems to have a different answer.

Wait for them to respond and then say,

That is exactly why everyone is so excited to come to a class. I have a few on the schedule. Pull out your calendar and let's get you plugged in.

STEP 3: SHARE

The better you become at the Share Cycle, the less often you will need to provide an oil experience. Nevertheless, sharing will always be a part of the cycle, because some people need a few experiences before they enroll. (Do yourself a favor and get a copy of the *Share dōTERRA* booklet from Share Success. It's a great resource to have on hand.)

Being prepared is 90 percent of sharing. Don't leave the house without your oils! How many times have you overheard someone complaining about an upset stomach, a headache, or a bout of insomnia, and you kicked yourself because you didn't have any samples.

Sharing begins with focusing 100 percent on helping the other person get the help they need right in the moment. I recommend giving out 31 samples in 31 days. You may be thinking that is a lot of money. Relax— you don't have to provide someone with 200 drops of Helichrysum! Give a person just 10 or so drops in a very small dram, teach them how to use the oil, and then ask, "What's the best way to contact you? I'll follow up with you in a few days to see how you are doing."

Your confidence will be that person's confidence, and if your heart is in the right place—that is, you really care about helping them—then you will eventually have a new fan!

STEP 4: INVITE

Step 4 is really the second part of contacting people and often occurs without your having to share a sample. The Invite step, in which you ask people to attend a class or one-on-one, is another opportunity to get a yes or a no. So naturally, it's also another opportunity to confront fear.

We feel uneasy about inviting someone to a class or one-on-one. Instead, we keep talking. Why?

We procrastinate about inviting people to a class because of fear. Fear that we will get a no. Fear that someone might say, "Is it network marketing?" Or, "Give me your card and I'll get back to you." Or, "How much are they?"

I've observed people doing what amounted to a mini-class, going through 47 different oils instead of simply asking the mom, "Based on what you just told me about your health goals and being open to having natural alternatives in your home, I feel you would love to visit one of my classes. I have one next Tuesday evening at 6:30 and one Thursday at 7:00. Which one would best fit your schedule—or would it be better for us to visit one-on-one this week?"

Have you ever had a great conversation with someone who seemed interested, but you did not have a class on the schedule to invite them to? This is a big reason why people have low invites. Make sure you have at least two classes on the schedule at all times so people can have an option. When you have something to invite people to, it's a lot easier to ask!

STEP 5: EXPLORE

The peppermint brownies are hot. The hummus with lemon is in the bowl. The people are arriving—and you are excited! You get everyone a few refreshments and jump right into teaching and passing around oils.

Too bad. You've just skipped over the step where 80 percent of all enrollment decisions occur—the Explore stage.

We have heard many times that the oils sell themselves. That is partly true; however, if you think that merely taking the top off a bottle of Lavender will make a credit card automatically appear, you might want to take a step back for a moment.

dōTERRA essential oils are indeed awesome. But there is a lot more going on behind the scenes of a sale or an enrollment than just the smell. That's why the Explore stage is vital and why you should never leapfrog over it and immediately start uncorking oils.

"Neal, that is crazy," you say. "These are the best oils in the world. They are CPTG®, and dōTERRA is simply an awesome company. All I need to do is let people experience the product, and sales and enrollments will be a breeze."

I only wish it were that easy. If this is your method of sharing and it works for you, awesome. However, why not invest a little more time to help the remaining 80 percent of people who might have enrolled had you gone through the Explore step before introducing the products.

People buy the problem before they buy the product. And then they don't really buy the product—they buy the feeling they get when they use the product. They buy how painful their headache is and how good it feels to get relief. They buy how burned out they feel after three sleepless nights and how wonderful it is to finally wake up refreshed.

That's the level we've got to speak on, and if we don't, we will lose good customers and potential wellness advocates.

The Explore stage is the emotional part of the class. It's is where decisions are made—because, remember, people justify their purchases with their logic, but they make them from their emotions. So when the emotional step gets skipped, is it any wonder that enrollment percentages drop, or that at the end of the class you hear, "I want to think about it" and "Let me talk to my spouse"?

There's yet another reason why the Explore stage is so critical to success: it's the stage where customer objections get answered before they even arise.

A principle in human interaction is that the first person to the objection wins. In other words, if you forget to talk about health professionals using essential oils, and if you fail to mention the doctors on your team who recommend oils to their patients, then at the end of the class, you may wind up with people who believe that doctors wouldn't approve of the products.

It's very difficult to turn people around once they've said, "I'm not comfortable enrolling until I talk to my doctor." And you can easily defuse that objection up front, at the beginning of the class, simply by saying that many doctors not only use essential oils but also recommend them to their patients. Then follow that up with a question: "Why do you feel so many doctors recommend them to their patients these days?" The answer they give you will likely be a reason they gain confidence in dōTERRA.

Never tell someone something you can get them to say for themselves. Their own answer will be more believable to them, and once they've said it, they will own it. Remember, people don't usually buy what you are selling; they buy what you can get them to say. Get them talking by mastering the art of asking questions.

Addressing customer challenges up front not only corrects people's faulty notions but also decreases people's fear of making a decision.

QUESTIONS ARE THE ANSWER

We need to master the art of asking questions in order to discover what is important to people. That discovery in turn helps us create an internal need for the products. Questions open people up to buying dōTERRA.

My first professional sales experience was at a house outside of Asheville, North Carolina, talking with a mom about some books that would help her with her kids. The manager I was with had me do the demonstration, and instead of asking questions, I immediately pulled out a book and started explaining the pages.

I kept talking and talking about the product, hoping that by doing so I could keep the customer from saying no. Finally, after the manager hit me in the arm several times with the order pad, I realized that the mom was ready to buy!

The point here is not that many people simply want to buy stuff from us (which was the case in this instance, because I was horrible), but that if we ask questions and discover what is important to the other person, then we know what to show. And we also know when we need to stop showing and begin signing people up!

CREATING A NEED

Many trainers discuss the importance of a product's features and benefits. You need to talk more about the benefits to people, they tell you—and it's true. Ultimately, people buy to alleviate pain (or create pleasure, to some extent). So if you fail to clearly understand their pain, you'll have a hard time getting them to part with their hard-earned money.

You have to create a need and reveal people's dissatisfaction with their current situation. I often tell people in my coaching and training courses, "Good sales people can find a need. Great salespeople can uncover needs. But STARfish *create* needs!"

Your success and significance are determined by many things. One of them is your ability to create a need. In direct selling (or sharing, as I call it), we are often introducing a product or service that the customer is not currently using. Because we are bringing it to them for the first time, we need to bear in mind that the customer does not know anything about the product and how it can benefit them.

Granted, it's good to talk about the benefit of using Lavender to support sleep. But that's just scratching the surface. If we don't help the customer understand the implications of sleep loss, a need will not be created, and hence an enrollment is less likely to occur.

The iPad is a hugely successful example of need creation. Before Apple came out with the iPad, how many of us were walking around saying, "I sure wish someone would invent a screen that didn't have a keyboard and a hinge. I can't get through life without one."

One person did come up with such a device. Steve Jobs understood that he could greatly improve the profitability of Apple by creating products that people were not aware they needed until *after* they were introduced to Apple's marketing plan and to the frenzy created by the early adopters who lined up to get the new device.

No one initially needed an iPad. Yet once it was introduced, Apple sold millions of them. That's because the existence of the iPad and what it could do for people created the need for it, and to such a degree that those who already had perfectly good iPads would wait for days in line to get the newest version. *That* is creating a need! Apple understood what was important to people.

Questions open people up, and they also take the focus off of us. If you ever feel nervous about what you are going to say, simply ask a question. People would rather hear what they have to say than what you've got to say!

What kinds of questions should you ask? Let the following ones serve as your guideline. When you know the answers to them *before* you begin talking about the products, your confidence will increase. And pressure will decrease, because people usually do not buy until they perceive there is a need. Asking good questions can help you create that need. Here are a few:

- What is their reality? (Where are they now?)
- What are their goals? (Where do they want to go?)
- What would they change?
- Why would change be important?
- Are you talking to the decision maker(s)?
- Ask questions that create vision: "If you could have more of what you want (health, energy, fitness) and less of what you don't want (fat, pain, toxins, expensive medical bills), is that something you would want to
  - check out?" (If contacting or inviting.)
  - use?" (If in a class.)

Knowing the answers to these six questions will quadruple the amount of people who enroll at your classes or one-on-ones.

Ever ask yourself during a class, "What is going on in their heads? Are they even interested?" Do you know their goals, concerns, issue and why it would be important to change?

In dōTERRA, we usually are talking to moms, and they are usually the decision maker when it comes to the products. But sometimes at the end of a class you'll encounter someone who says she has to talk to her spouse—and she really does. She won't make any financial decision on her own.

Had you known that both parties needed to be part of the decision to enroll, you could have simply invited the spouse to the class. But many times we don't learn about that part of the equation until after the fact. So we need to assure attendees up front that the decision to enroll with dōTERRA is one that most wives feel comfortable making because most of the husbands tell them it's their department. Think about it. When the kids get a boo-boo, to whom do they run? Take it from me, it's usually *not* Dad.

When you help people create a vision for what could be you have a solid chance for them to buy into your vision. When you know where they are and where they want to go and then paint that picture in their minds, they develop confidence: "So if you could get in better shape and have more energy, is that something you would want to check out?"

One of the ways in which to create a need is to have people go through the Wellness Lifestyle Triangle™. It looks like the chart on the next page.

Asking people to score themselves on a scale of 1 to 10 in each of the areas will immediately create a little pain. (It did for me the first

time I did it.) That discomfort sparks discussion, and you can then begin to ask some questions:

- Why do you feel so many people are into natural alternatives these days?
- Why would it be important to score above an 8 or 9 on all levels of the Wellness Triangle?
- How would you feel if you could move your scores up a few numbers?
- What do you feel will happen if you don't reach your wellness goals?

Remember that the answer is inside them. You simply need to ask the right questions and be willing to listen and then process the answers.

STEP 6: TEACH

Now comes the fun part. We get to finally talk about the products! As mentioned earlier, approximately 80 percent of the buying decision has been made by this point in the class. Teaching is simply demonstrating how your product will solve people's problems. This is the part in which we educate and motivate people to do what is best for them.

Chances are good that you will be teaching a Reinventing Healthcare class in which you talk about the current state of our healthcare system, share your story, and discuss how essential oils and other products can be used as natural alternatives to traditional medicine.

One of the traps presenters often fall into is to describe products by their use alone: "This is Peppermint; people use it to cool their body temperature when they are hot. This is Lavender; you use it to support healthy sleep."

That's intriguing to an extent, but there's a more effective way. Here is a little system that will help you build interest, create in people a dissatisfaction with where they're at, and speak to the emotional part of the brain (as discussed in chapter 6).

A.T.T.S.

> **A**—Ask a question.
> **T**—"Tell me about that."
> **T**—Tell a third-person story.
> **S**—Show an oil/product/solution.

Here is an example of how this system could play out in a class.

ASK A QUESTION

First, ask, "How many people have ever had trouble going to sleep or known someone who did?"

Notice how I added "or known someone who did." Here you don't want to ask a question to which you don't know the answer. If you ask only the first part, it is possible that no one will have had that issue, and then you're stuck. But everyone these days knows at least *someone* who has sleeping issues.

"TELL ME ABOUT THAT"

When you get the answer, resist the temptation to jump directly into talking about the solution. Give people a chance to stew for a bit in their dissatisfaction in order to create a need. Remember, people don't buy the product until they buy that there is a problem.

By saying, "Tell me about that," you can take people back to the exact time when they tossed and turned and couldn't fall asleep. Keep asking questions such as, "How did that affect you the next day? And then what happened?" You want them to vividly recall, in the class, how frustrated they felt when they were tossing and turning in their bed two nights ago—because that frustration and the burnout of sleep deprivation are the things they want to, and *can*, change.

TELL A THIRD-PERSON STORY

Next you share an anecdote. Third-person stories are powerful for a couple reasons. First, people believe 25 percent of what you say, but they believe 75 percent of what you can get *them or others to* say. Second, telling the story of someone else who had the problem under discussion, and who found its solution by using the product, will increase confidence and help ease the fear of making a buying decision.

Picture yourself in a grocery store, trying to choose between different breakfast cereals. You are comparing the ingredients, the cost per ounce—and then someone standing beside you says, "My kids love that cereal." What do you do? Exactly. You put that cereal in the cart. The helpful shopper helped you decide *and* took most of the risk out of making the decision (because now you can blame someone else if the kids don't like it!).

Gather as many third-person stories as you can. You should have a third-person story for every possible customer challenge (objection) and for most of the products you will show in a class. As you progress in your business, you will want to have a story for every product.

Here is how telling a third-person story might work. Someone has just told you about their bout of insomnia. In response, you say, "That's what Erin told me just the other day. She said, 'I have trouble sleeping, and it seems to affect the rest of my day if not the rest of my week.'"

SHOW AN OIL/PRODUCT/SOLUTION

Now it's time to introduce the solution: "And that is why Erin loves using Lavender before bedtime. She puts it on the bottom of her feet and even diffuses it. That's another reason she made sure she got the diffuser—so she could support her sleep *topically* as well as *aromatically*."

Then you want to ask another question, such as, "Makes sense doesn't it?" or "Can you see why she was excited to have these oils in her home?"

Third-person stories are powerful and should be used in every Share Cycle step, from contacting through follow-up.

IT'S A DIALOGUE, NOT A MONOLOGUE

Have you ever felt like you were doing all of the talking in a class? An hour of monologue can be uncomfortable not only for us but for our guests as well.

Asking questions throughout the class not only creates a dialogue but also helps us know where people are on the buying line. For example, when we ask, "Makes sense, doesn't it?" we are taking people's temperature so we can see who is with us and who might be daydreaming. Here are some questions you can use:

"What do you feel you would use the most so far, Judy?"

"Sally, what has been your favorite part of the class so far?"

"Can you begin to see why so many doctors are now using this with their patients?"

"How would you use this at home with *your* kids?"

"How do you see using dōTERRA in your home benefitting our family."

After receiving the answer to a question, you can simply say, "That is what most people have been telling me—and I feel it is why so many people have been excited to use this stuff. One mom said, 'It just makes logical sense to have this around the house.'"

Remember, the answers your attendees provide can be used by you during the enrollment step to remind them of the importance of having the products in their home!

10 TIPS FOR TEACHING WITH INSPIRATION

1. Take control.
2. Follow a script.
3. Always speak to a set of eyes

4. Move with purpose.
5. Use voice inflection. Avoid monotone.
6. Focus on body language and eliminate distractions.
7. Follow the A.T.T.S. formula. And remember, sharing comes *last*.
8. Use people's names.
9. Avoid *ums* and useless words.
10. Record your class.

STEP 7: SUMMARIZE

After sitting for an hour, people often forget what you covered in the class. Imagine how another person feels trying to digest in 45 minutes the information that took you a month to understand!

So it's vital that you summarize the content, including any aha! moments during the class. Then begin to ask some opening (the old school term is *closing*) questions.

The following questions help people focus on the important points they may have gleaned from the class. They also help you take the class's temperature before you ask them to make an enrollment decision.

What did you like best about the class? Was it when we talked about saving money? Or about how you would have safer, more effective options right at home?

Why do you feel your husbands would be so excited to get these in your homes: because it would save your family money in the long run, or because the products would help support health goals—or both?

If you were 100 percent sure, beyond a shadow of a doubt, that you would experience one of your health challenges within the next month, and you already had these products in your home, how would you feel?

You will see the last question in the next section as well.

STEP 8: CLOSING IS OPENING

For most people, closing is a dirty word. So we will use the term *open*. Open people up to getting some really great products. Open them up to a future revenue stream. Open them up to making a decision that is best for them.

What comes to your mind when you think about the word *closing*? Do you start to get cold sweats? Are you thinking about the last time you purchased a new or used car? No one likes to be pressure-closed. However, people *need* someone to help them make a decision. In fact, that is your job as a STARfish!

If we are doing our part correctly, we will be viewed as the expert. This is one of the main differences between the direct selling model and the retail environment: In order for a sale to occur, direct selling requires well-informed consultants to educate the customer about the product. People need to understand our product before they will buy it.

So we in turn must understand the challenges that people go through when making a buying decision. Our job as a STARfish is to help people process the education they receive in a class and ultimately make a decision that is best for themselves and their families. We need to help them get a vision of their need, because they may not see it unassisted. Most people cannot do these things on their own. Otherwise, they would simply go to a retail store.

Making decisions can be scary! People do not want to make the wrong decision, so they make no decision at all. We do them a service by helping them get past their sticking point to make the decision that is best for them. If you have ever struggled with a decision and then had someone help you through it, you know what I mean.

Our goal is not to pressure people into getting what we have so we can get an enrollment, win some trip, or advance in rank. Save that for the SELLfish. However, be aware that chemical and biological changes occur in people when they are in a decision making mode, and these are enhanced when they perceive that we are there expecting an answer. STARfish seek to help people get past the physiological barriers that can hamper their ability to make wise choices. You may not think of it in those terms, and you don't need to, but it's part of what occurs during a well-conducted close.

So remember: Closing is not something you do *to* people; it's something you do *for* people. Closing is simply the step in the Share Cycle where it's time for people to make a decision and then move on. Closing is opening people to the possibilities of having dōTERRA in their homes.

In fact, *not* closing is more pressure. Think about it. When someone leaves your class after telling you they want to "think about it," now you have to call them back: "Hey, it's Neal, and I'm just calling to see if you made a decision." That is pressure!

Or they "need to go home and talk to their husband" when in fact they could have made the decision on their own had we handled their concern in the class. Now we have to play telephone tag to get their answer. Have you ever had someone go into the witness protection program to avoid returning your calls?

Closing is not one question but rather a sequence of questions. Think of it as a series of green lights. You ask a question like, "Can you see how using Peppermint could have helped a few times last week?" and wait for the response. If it's yes, then you can go on with the process. If it's no, then you know you have some work to do.

Closing is actually a lot of fun if you know how to do it correctly. Unfortunately, most people do not close correctly and end up putting more pressure on people than if they simply did it the right way. Many people avoid this stage like the plague because they don't want to come off as pushy. So here is a question: Would you feel bummed out if someone had not shared dōTERRA with you? Exactly! Now pass on the favor by doing everything you can to help others have the same best shot at enrolling. That includes helping them make decisions.

Picture someone sitting on the couch shuffling paperwork. To you they may appear focused and decisive, but in reality they are calling out for help. They are saying "I don't know what I need or what I want. This is all new to me. I need someone with experience to help me decide what to do." People usually do not close themselves. Yet at the end of the class, many wellness advocates say something like, "Let me know if you have any questions, and feel free to grab some more peppermint brownies and hummus." We think people will automatically fill out the form. I wish it were that easy.

Don't buy the lie that doing anything more than volunteering to answer questions is being pushy. In reality, not sitting down with them and helping them make a decision creates more pressure. People have a difficult time making decisions without your assistance.

You can feel the quiet in the room when a person is making a decision. You feel the pressure as you watch them shuffle their class materials and order form. Here are a some questions you can ask to help them along.

> If you were 100 percent sure, beyond a shadow of a doubt, that you would experience one of your health concerns within the next month, and you already had these products in your home, how would you feel?

> If this could easily fit in your budget and not take food off your table, would there be anything that would prevent you from getting started tonight?

> If you had access to safer, cheaper, and more effective healthcare options in your home, would that be a good thing?

Now you are ready to help people decide if what they just experienced is for them.

SHARE AN EMOTIONAL STORY

Emotional stories help take people from the technical part of the class to the emotional aspect of making a decision. If you ever hear, "I want to think about it," at the end of a class or one-on-one, then you were likely talking to that person's logical part of their brain, and as a result, she is now finding it difficult to make a decision. That's why an emotional story is a vital tool for priming the decision making process.

Here is an example of a third-person, emotional story, told in a way that can help people focus on what is really important and why they would want to enroll.

> As Peggy said, insurance is expensive to purchase but even more to use. You have copays, out-of-pocket deductibles, and premiums. So

while a lot of people think these products might be expensive, they actually fit into everyone's budget.

It's like Suzie told me the other night: "We spend more money on things for the kids, video games, eating out, toys, and cell phone charges, so it made perfect sense to have something like this around the house when we need it!" Plus, she felt she could save a bundle in medical costs by promoting a healthy lifestyle, so she had her family take supplements every day. That's why she wanted to enroll.

GROUP CLOSE

Here is a sample script for a group close:

By a show of hands, how many of you picked up a few things you are going to be able to use? Great! Who would like to spend some time learning about how to use these products on an ongoing basis?

Well, I'm sure you can see the value this would bring to your family, and you are likely wondering if it's for you. Ask yourself three questions: First, do you want safer, cheaper, more effective options to support your health? Second, do you want a healthier lifestyle for you and your family? Third, have you thought several times over the past year that it would be helpful to have quality health-supporting products in your home?

If you said no to any of these three questions, then we know that this would probably not be a fit for you, and that is totally okay.

Let me go ahead and talk about a few of the most common questions. First, How much is it? Well, that depends on what you get. Most people get either the Diamond Kit, the Every Oil Kit, the Natural Solutions Kit, or the Home Essentials Kit. It all depends on your budget. Most people want to get the biggest kit they can afford without taking food off of the table, because that is the most intelligent way to buy—and the membership is included.

When you compare the cost of healthcare, doctor visits, premiums, copays, and deductibles, it's about a third of what you pay monthly for health insurance. But there is something for everyone. We have college students buying this, so don't worry.

Second, let's say you know you want to do this, but it's bad timing. If that is the case, we can definitely work something out for you to make sure you can get started if you want to.

Third, you know you want to do this, but you have to talk to your spouse. Of course you want to talk to your spouse, and I promise you we don't want to cause any family squabbles or have anyone sleeping on the couch! But what I do know for sure is that if you know this will help you and your family, and you are committed to using these products, then you will convince whoever you need to convince in order to make it happen.

Most moms tell us that they are the ones who will use dōTERRA the most, and their spouse would be pretty excited if he had a safer, cheaper, and more effective option to hauling the kids to the doctor and getting a big bill for something that could have been handled right at home for pennies per drop.

THREE CATEGORIES

So I'm going to hand out the enrollment forms. Don't worry—touching them won't charge your credit card!

By now you are in one of three different groups. The first group says, I'm in. You had me at hello. I love this stuff and can totally see myself using this. For people in this group, simply start filling out the shaded areas, choose a kit, and we will get you started right away.

The second group says, I want to do this but I have a few questions. If this is you, go ahead and fill out the form, and then you and I will visit *one-on-one, and we'll get your questions answered and pick out a kit that's right for you.*

If you are in the third group, you had a great time and learned a lot, but it's not for you. That is totally fine. But you may have had three or four people come to mind during the class who would enjoy coming to a future class. If you could just jot down their contact info, we will make sure we plug them into the next set of classes.

STEP 9: ENROLL

You have explained to people how they can become involved. They understand the loyalty reward program. Now it's time to sign them up! This can be the most difficult part. It's the step in the Share Cycle where presenters lose enrollments because they do not understand how people make decisions.

Many presenters tell me they simply finish explaining the kits and LRP and then say, "If you have any questions, just let me know." But again, people have a difficult time making decisions on their own, especially when the information is new to them. So we need to help attendees make a decision.

We do this by taking action and going directly to the most interested person in the room. Our confidence will be the confidence they will need when making a decision.

dōTERRA master wellness advocate and Double Diamond Justin Harrison recommends asking the following three questions:

1. "How did you *feel* about what you just experienced?"
2. "Would it be okay if I shared with you how to set up a wholesale membership?"
3. "Which of these options makes the most sense for your family and you?"

SOLIDIFY THE ENROLLMENT

Once you've made an enrollment, make sure you solidify it. This is where a lot of folks miss the ball: they fail to understand that people can develop buyer's remorse after making a decision.

How often have you pulled something off the shelf at the grocery store, put it in your cart, and then a few aisles later said to yourself, "You know what? I don't need this." We are good at talking ourselves out of things that often are good for us (and bad at talking ourselves out of things that are bad for us).

We need to be mindful of the situation that awaits enrollees when they get home. They may have a husband who is not happy that his wife went to our class in the first place. Maybe he had to put the kids to bed solo, and now he has to endure his wife's show-and-tell the minute she comes home—and usually, none of it is for him!

Here is typical post-class conversation between spouses:

"Hi, honey! I'm back from the class."

"Uh . . . you didn't buy anything did you?"

"Well, um . . . kind of."

"What did you get this time?"

"Just some essential oils."

"Oils? We don't need oils. You know we have a medical plan and you can go to the doctor. You don't believe in all that snake oil stuff, do you? Why did you get oils?"

"Well, I'm, uh, not sure . . . except, well, they are natural—and certified."

Okay, I've put you through enough. You know the drill. We need to empower people with the information they need to build their confidence, so their spouse does not derail the enrollment. Because the bottom line is, enrollees are trying to help their families.

A way to build confidence and solidify the enrollment is to ask the person, "Why did you end up enrolling tonight?" As she responds, have her write down her answers on her class handout while you take notes as well. That way, when she goes home, she can read exactly why she enrolled to her spouse. And better yet, you now have her reasons to use as a third-party testimonial—as well as backup in case she gets cold feet after entering the husband zone!

The wellness consult also validates the decision to buy. Set an appointment at the class or the following day to do the wellness consult with your new wellness advocate.

WHY PEOPLE EXPERIENCE BUYER'S REMORSE

Here are some common reasons why people have second thoughts about their purchase or enrollment:

- We didn't close in the buying zone
- Our class was *toooo* long.
- We didn't build a sharing environment.
- We forgot to say, "I just have to ask, Betty: Why did you decide to do this?"
- We didn't write down their reasons for enrolling on their enrollment form and take a picture of it so they could repeat those reasons back to their spouses.
- We didn't do a wellness consult.

STEP 10:FOLLOW-UP/REFERRALS

Some people will enroll. Some people will not enroll. What do we do with these two groups after the class?

FOLLOW-UP

You may have heard the saying "The fortune is in the follow-up." Do you have a good follow up plan?

The following striking statistics dramatize the importance of follow-up:

- 48 percent of salespeople never follow up with a prospect.
- 25 percent of salespeople make a second contact and stop.
- 12 percent of salespeople only make three contacts and stop.
- Only 10 percent of salespeople make more than three contacts.
- 2 percent of sales are made on the first contact.
- 3 percent of sales are made on the second contact.
- 5 percent of sales are made on the third contact.
- 10 percent of sales are made on the fourth contact.
- 80 percent of sales are made on the fifth to twelfth contact.

If this plays out as indicated, then we are all leaving a ton of enrollments on the table! According to these statistics, most people do not follow up. That is human nature. STARfish prioritize follow-up in order to increase their chances of securing an enrollment. I would argue that the above stats reflect people who have not learned the skills and mindset you are learning by reading this book—and the lower the level of skill, the more essential follow-up becomes.

TOP REASONS FOR FOLLOW-UP

Here are the top nine reasons why follow-up is so important. Do any of them look familiar?

1. People had to leave early.
2. People had to leave before they met one-on-one.
3. Needed to talk with husband/spouse.
4. Needed to think about it.
5. "It's a bad time. Call me next month."
6. They ordered retail.
7. They wanted to think about what to order.
8. The person wanted to check with their doctor.
9. They enrolled! (And you want them to stay enrolled.)

You will want to create two follow-up checklists: one for when people enroll and the other for when they do not.

Checklist for when people enroll

☐ Send a handwritten thank-you note.
☐ Make a "Welcome!" phone call.
☐ Send a "Welcome!" email with product education links.
☐ Do a wellness consult.
☐ Have a "three pathways" conversation.
☐ Invite them to attend a second class.
☐ Invite them to a maximizing membership class/webinar.
☐ Conduct an opportunity overview.
☐ Wellness Advocate Creed™.
☐ Builder worksheet.
☐ Success Challenge/Share. Lead. Inspire.
☐ Attend a Share. Lead. Inspire retreat.

☐ How to run a business training.

☐ How to inspire a team (leadership training).

☐ Attend team leaders retreat.

Checklist for when people do not enroll

☐ Know the *real* reason why before they leave class.

☐ Know their time frame for making a decision.

☐ Set a follow-up appointment at the class and put in their calendar.

☐ Write a handwritten thank-you note.

☐ Follow up with education and inspiration.

☐ Expect them to become customers, and believe in them!

REFERRALS

How many referrals do you get after the class? How about during a wellness consult? When is the best time to ask? Why don't more people ask for them?

You got to the end of the class, you provided value, and yet some folks discovered it was not for them and left without enrolling. No problem, right?

Wrong. When people walk out of a class or one-on-one, anywhere from 25 to 600 other people leave with them. I once read that the average person knows 600 people and has between 10 and 25 people they trust in their network. So let's just arbitrarily choose the number 15 and multiply it by the number of people who left your last class without enrolling. *That is the number of potential customers you could have!* Suppose that five people leave. There are potentially 75 people who trust those five and who are great candidates for your next class!

What about those who do enroll? The number goes up due to the credibility of the referral. So if you have 10 people at a class who enroll, then there are potentially 150 other people who could be introduced to you by enrollees whom they know and trust.

Referrals are vital in your business. People buy when someone they trust reduces or eliminates the risk of purchasing from the buyer's mind. That is why third-party testimonials and stories are key. It is powerful to hear a story of someone who has had a great product experience.

So why do people avoid asking for referrals? It starts with their belief system. The word *referrals* carries a negative connotation. Many people may picture an insurance salesman hammering at them for the names of all of their friends, whom the salesman wants to high-pressure into buying a policy. To avoid that negative association, while we will use the word *referral* in our discussion, you should not use it when you are talking with a customer or prospect.

WHY PEOPLE DON'T ASK FOR REFERRALS

Any or all of several factors can play into people's reluctance to ask for referrals.

They may not believe that a customer who just enrolled will share the names of their friends until *after* they have had a chance to experience the product for themselves.

They may fear that they'll mess up the sale. As one wellness advocate said, "I just had them sit through an hour-and-a-half class and agree to purchase a kit. I don't want to come across as pushy now and ask them for all of their friends' names."

They're afraid of touching a nerve with a customer who had a bad experience referring someone else to a friend. Let's say the vacuum cleaner salesman stopped by your customer's house two months ago, and the customer referred them to her sister, and the sister subsequently chewed out your customer for making the referral. She might have cold feet about giving another referral—and you might feel reluctant to risk asking for one.

The customer may not view sharing a referral as helping her friends. She needs to become convinced that she is doing them a good turn by helping them gain access to something that helped her. The referral-asking game can be filled with pressure if your customers focus on themselves rather than on helping their friends get the same great benefit (education at the class) that they have just experienced.

Finally, some people just can't think of anyone. Or if they do pass on the name of someone they know, they request that you not use their own name. That is not a referral.

Those are the obstacles; now how do we move beyond them and get referrals? It starts with getting into the right mindset. We have to believe that our customers will like us, that they will trust us, and that we can deliver an equally high level of service to their referrals. And we have to believe in our mission. It's our duty to help people help their friends acquire healthcare solutions that can change their lives.

Have you ever taught a great class and had plenty of enrollments, but the next day you had to start all over because you exhausted all of your names? Referrals are an easy way to open up the conversation, take the pressure off yourself, and begin to help people help their friends.

Some of your best customers will come from people who didn't enroll or even come to a class—but they did refer their friends. For that matter, I've had people refer their friends and in the process talk themselves into either coming to a class or enrolling!

SIMPLE BRIDGE STATEMENT FOR REQUESTING A REFERRAL

Use the following script as a model for requesting referrals from your customers.

> Betty, I really appreciate working with you tonight, and I know you will love your kit.
>
> Many of the people who come to our classes get about 10 minutes in and think of several friends or family members who would also have loved to be here tonight. As a professional courtesy to people who come to my classes, we set up a class for their friends who would have wanted to come.
>
> So Betty, did anyone you know come to mind during the class—friends, family, or whomever—who are just like you and whom we should be talking to? You know—they want a safer, cheaper, and more effective option, just like you do?

You may need to jog their memory. People often cannot remember other people on the spot, so we need to open up their minds. Following is another brief script to guide you.

> As I said in the beginning of the class, people come to these classes for one of three reasons. First, they are already into natural alternatives. Or second, they don't like the side effects of a prescription or supplement, or they don't like what their doctor is recommending. Or third, they are dealing with changes in healthcare. Perhaps their copay has increased, or their insurance has a high deductible, or their doctor is no longer in the network. In any case, they want to create their first line of defense at home.
>
> So, who comes to mind that we can help as well?

You can also offer suggestions: fellow church members, women in their moms' group, their massage therapist, their chiropractor, and so forth.

CHAPTER 8

CUSTOMER CHALLENGES

With man this is impossible,
but with God all things are possible.

—Matthew 19:26

STARfish know how to handle customer challenges. It is critical that we address potential challenges before they arise. Remember, the first one to the objection wins!

People avoid making a decision because they fear making the wrong decision. They will use any excuse they can find to protect them from the pain of going home from a class and being bombarded by a husband: "We don't need oils—we have health insurance." Or, "You didn't get suckered into buying any of that snake oil, did you?"

FOUR MAIN OBJECTION AREAS

It's helpful to know that people's objections group into just four categories. Once you recognize them, you can know how to address them. They are these:

- Status quo: the customer is happy with their current product.
- Price: the product costs too much money.

- Spouse: a husband or wife opposes the purchase.
- Procrastination: the customer wants to think about it.

By factoring these objections into how we structure our class, we can deal with them proactively. For instance, we can inform our class how many of the people using dōTERRA had previously been using another company's oils. We can reassure them that one of the main reasons people love using essential oils, and especially dōTERRA essential oils, is because *everyone* can afford them.

We need to include a segment in the class that shows what men love about dōTERRA, and we should include products in our presentation that men use daily. Third-party stories are key in this segment.

What about objections during the Contact stage or at the end of a class? Let's say you get to the end of the class and someone says, "That is a lot of money." In the old-school way of handling objections, the salesperson would attempt to identify with the person's feelings: "I understand how you *feel*. I *felt* the same way until I realized that oils cost pennies per drop and actually save you money."

Today many people easily recognize this tactic, and it usually comes across as insincere. If you and I just met 45 minutes ago, how can I really understand how you feel? It's a bit presumptuous to say you do, especially if you're a man talking to a woman!

One of the quickest ways to lose credibility is to tell someone you understand their feelings when in fact you don't have a clue how they feel—because you haven't asked them! Besides, people don't care how *you* felt. You are the salesperson, and they automatically distrust you because you benefit if they buy into your pitch.

The following is a better system for taking the pressure off and being authentic.

6 STEPS TO ADDRESSING OBJECTIONS

1. Focus on the benefit for the customer.
2. Identify the real issue.
3. Use a bridge statement.
4. Use third-person "feeling" statement.
5. Use a third person to address the objection.
6. Point out how health challenge and so forth can be addressed with the product.
7. Close.

Following are some scripts that illustrate how you might handle various objections.

HAPPY WITH THE CURRENT PRODUCT

When people tell you they already use another oil company or are looking at one, or they ask, "How are you different," they are really saying, "Help me make a decision." We tend to go on about CPTG, sourcing, culture, and how great we are rather than focusing on the customer. Next time, try this instead:

Mrs. Customer, I know you are evaluating the best options for your family, and I really can appreciate that. Sally Johnson said this same thing last week, and what she really wanted was some criteria that she should be using to evaluate her best option.

What I said to her was, "You will want to make sure that the oils are sourced from the best place in which to grow and harvest each plant. We have found through extensive research that this is one of the keys to potency. We could just grow them on a big farm or two here in the U.S., but that would not be the best for our customers.

"Next, you will want to make sure that they have a CPTG stamp to ensure purity and integrity according to third-party testing.

"Finally, you will want a company that provides a holistic, big-picture approach to health and wellness by having products that address concerns that go beyond just those for which you would use oils. For example, you will want access to a great cleansing product to remove existing toxins from your body and optimize organ function. You want products that help you reduce toxic load and ones that support nutrition, so you ultimately need less oils!

"When you have all of those things working together, then you have the best chance to achieve optimum health. Without those key elements, essential oils are simply not as effective. And our mission to provide not only the highest quality essential oils but also to help people optimize their overall health, so they can do more of what they love to do with more energy and less stress."

And that is why everyone has been so excited about dōTERRA!

Have fun with using this script—and remember to have a humble heart!

YOUR COMPANY CPTG STANDARD IS JUST A MARKETING PLOY

You: *Why do you feel dōTERRA had to create a standard?*

Prospect: *Because there wasn't one?*

You: *Exactly right. dōTERRA knew that there was a better way that did not currently exist, so they created their own standard. Their mission is to have the purest essential oils available on the planet. They wanted to be able to test those oils to make sure they were indeed pure. There are many things that go into that standard, including third-party testing.*

But let's just say it is a marketing scheme. Why in the world, then, would dōTERRA source their oils from all over the world? Why not just copy what others do and grow them in Utah, add fillers, and still use the CPTG label. I mean, it is theirs to use right? They made it up!

Prospect: *That sort of makes sense*

You: *Which would be more expensive for dōTERRA: to get each of their oils from a different the place in the world according to where it is the most potent, or to just have one big farm and grow all of the plants in the same place?*

Prospect: *It would be cheaper to grow them all in one place.*

You: *So the only logical conclusion is that this standard is far from marketing and more about dōTERRA being true to its mission of having the purest and most potent essential oils on the planet. That's what is best for the customer. And that's what the CPTG standard means.*

I mean, I can use any essential oil I want. But dōTERRA essential oils are the only essential oils I will put on my kids, because they are safe, pure, and potent.

MONEY

Prospect: *That costs a lot of money.*

You: *I totally get it. A lot of people are pinching pennies these days and want to make sure they are spending money only on necessities. They hold off on buying things they don't need.*

Let me ask you this: Besides it being "a lot of money," is there any other reason that keeps you from enrolling?

Prospect: *No, it's just the money.*

You: *Oh, good. Jenny felt pretty much the same way. She said that she and her husband are cutting a lot out of the budget and trying to save money these days. One of the reasons she ended up enrolling is because she wanted to make sure she had something around the house that would save them money in the long run, because she said just a doctor visit can be a few hundred dollars,—not counting the time getting to the doctor, time in the waiting room, and the chance that the other kids or she herself could catch something while she was there.*

She said she wasn't sure she had the money, but one thing was for sure: she wanted to be prepared so she didn't have to spend more money down the road if the kids got sick or developed symptoms and she didn't know what to do. She said one doctor visit could cost as much as one of the kits. How do you think she feels now, having these oils in her house?

Prospect: *Safer, I guess. Ready to handle upcoming health challenges.*

You: *Exactly! That's the main reason everyone has been so excited about dōTERRA. So lets go ahead and get you started.*

Or try this:

I can totally get where you are coming from. You do a great job of making sure you know where your money is going. Besides feeling like you don't have it in the budget, is there anything else that would prevent you from using the products? . . .

Well, you are not alone. However, a lot of folks we work with understand that investing in (name of products/oils) will actually end up saving them money, because they can be used as a first line of defense when a family member gets sick or has a need.

Betty Johnson said she couldn't afford the oils at first, but when she did the math, it totally changed her mind. She said it makes logical sense to have something like this around the house, because it was not a matter of if something was going to happen—it was a matter of when. And she not only wanted to make sure she was prepared for the little emergencies, but she also wanted to take her family's healthcare into her own hands.

So can you see how this kit would help with your health concerns and goals—and it can actually save you money in medical expenses? Great! Would it be okay with if I share with you how to set up your wholesale membership?

SPOUSE

I hear you completely. Besides wanting to talk to your spouse, is there any other reason keeping you from enrolling?

Most of the moms are the ones who end up making the decision to get oils. One mom said that when the kids get sick or fall down, they usually run to her. Yes, sometimes it's Dad, but usually it's Mom. She said she is the one who makes the decision when it comes to buying things for the kids. She is the one who writes the check for the doctor visit, prescription drugs, and just getting Band-Aids at the drug store.

Dad, on the other hand, usually takes care of his things. She said, "If he blows a tire on the way home from work or needs a new lawnmower, we don't have a family meeting to see if he is going to get a new tire or lawnmower. He simply goes and gets one. It's his department, and I trust his decision that he will get the best tire or lawnmower. And he trusts that on my part, I will also make the best decision when evaluating things to take care of the family."

PROCRASTINATION

I totally get where you are coming from. Besides wanting to think about it, is there any other reason keeping you from enrolling tonight?

Most people want to think about what they are doing to make sure they are making the best decision. We all want to make sure we are getting what we need and will use.

Based on your wellness wish list, which of your health goals did you want to work on first? Why did you pick those two? If there were a kit that would help with those, would that be a good thing? Why?

Based on what you've told me, it sounds like (name the appropriate kit) is going to be a perfect fit for you. Go ahead and fill in your information and check this box for the kit, and we will get it sent out tomorrow.

MLM CHALLENGE

I have so enjoyed this conversation and feedback! And I agree with a lot of what you've had to say. Mind if I share a few of my own perspectives?

MLMs of today are very different from those of our parents' generation. The legitimate ones are not a get-rich-quick scheme but are based on service and consumption. What I mean is, they give you the option to buy something unique from another person, often another mom like yourself, rather than from a big box store. You get an equal, and often superior, product from the mom. Kind of like the whole concept of buying local.

The struggle comes into play when salespeople act like fire hoses, spewing information and their product all over their Facebook page or every conversation you have with them. That's why I personally swore I would never be a part of an MLM.

But I found a product I love and use every day, and that gives me the opportunity to truly help other people by sharing it with them.

In just two years, I have been able to completely replace my husband's corporate six-figure income and enabled him to come work with me full-time.

Now we do this as a family, helping to empower and transform other people's health and finances. It has allowed me to stay at home with our kids.

Before I had kids, I was an executive recruiter. We would never have hired an accountant who didn't have accounting experience or a lawyer without a law degree. If you don't have some business or sales background and want to supplement your income with an MLM or any sales job, then you should learn some basic sales skills. And you can learn them—but you have to put forth the effort.

Whether you realize it or not, we are all in network marketing to some degree It's just that very few people get paid for it. How many times have you asked your waitress what her favorite dish is? Or asked someone for a great book suggestion? How about a good movie? You were going to eat a meal, read a book, and see a movie regardless of what they said, but their recommendation influenced your choice. However, none of them got compensated for sharing with you what they enjoyed. That's just not how the restaurant, bookstore, and movie theaters are set up.

For all the mommies who are part of an MLM and don't want to be that friend whom people run from: have a heart of service. When your heart is on service, you cannot be nervous. I would rather mention what I do, educate people on alternatives, and have people say no than to never say anything at all. I consider myself the messenger, and what others do with that information is up to them.

This last, heartfelt scenario comes to you courtesy of Erin Anderson, my wife.

ASSIGNMENT

1. Write out answers to most common objections.
2. Find third-party testimonials of people who overcame these objections.
3. Practice these with someone and commit them to memory.

BECOMING THE
INSPIREfish™

I t was a year later, and once again Sellfy was sitting across from Sherri in her office. But what a difference that year had made! A difference in Sellfy's volume, beyond a doubt, but most of all, a difference in Sellfy.

Sherri smiled at him. "I wonder if you have any idea just how much you've changed, Sellfy. That guy who walked in here a year back was broken and yet prideful. The man I'm looking at now is confident yet humble. And, I might add, servant-hearted—and successful."

It was true. Following all of the principles Sherri had guided him through, Sellfy had transformed his business and had a wonderful time in the process. People were now drawn to Sellfy. He loved how he was changing lives by helping people find a safer, cheaper, and more effective form of healthcare. He loved making a real difference. Sellfy was no longer a SELLfish. He had become Sellfy the STARfish!

"I couldn't have done it without you, Sherri," he gratefully admitted. "I owe you so much."

"You owe me nothing except to pass on the blessing," Sherri replied. "You're ready. You became coachable. You worked hard. And you understand that there are no shortcuts, just a system that works if you follow it."

"It sure does," Sellfy said. "And I'm amazed how much fun it's been. I would love to help others learn how to do what I do. I can't imagine anything more rewarding than watching them grow and reach for their dreams. So how do I go about it?"

"It's time to get you into the leadership program. Time to help you inspire a team and change their lives just like yours has been changed. Meet me back here on April 26th, 2015, and we will get to work."

Sherri's smile broadened. "Until then, Mr. STARfish, go change the world one drop, one person, one family at a time."

APPENDIX

STARFISH

- Extremely coachable
- Works a schedule
- Extremely positive
- Leads with product
- Focuses on sowing
- Focuses on activity
- Asks questions to find a need
- Creates a sharing environment
- Has a vision for their life
- Finds a way
- Welcomes coaching
- Controls the controllables
- Leaves everyone in a great mood
- Uses 3rd person stories
- Invests back into their business
- Knows and applies the Share Cycle™
- Always finds out, "How did you hear about dōTERRA?

SELLFISH

- Knows it all
- Wings it
- Glass is half empty
- Leads with opportunity
- Focuses on selling
- Focuses on sales
- Knows it all
- Creates pressure
- Has no long-term vision
- Finds an excuse
- On an island
- Focuses on things they can't control
- Is frustrated with rejection
- Uses their stories
- Complains about investing in business
- Uses their "own" system
- Cross recruits/enrolls other people's people

ACKNOWLEDGEMENTS

I felt an intense sense of accomplishment when I finished my last edit. There had been many sleepless nights, missed meals, nights I did not read with my kids or have dinner with my wife. Now the book is finished, and it's time to say a few thank-yous. I have ample reasons to feel grateful toward a number of people in my life.

Before I thank those people specifically, though, I want to say thanks to all of the people behind the tens of thousands of doors on which I have knocked. Your yeses paid my bills. Your noes built my character. Without the opportunities you gave me to face my fears during those 50,000 sales calls, I would not be who I am today. You were my laboratory of life. You allowed me to gain a unique perspective by meeting with you in your living rooms, on your front porches, under carports, and in your offices. Thank you.

Thank you to my friends at Southwestern Advantage who gave me an opportunity back as a college student to knock on all of those doors: Dan Moore, Craig Soeder, Jason Fox, Michael Jones, Aaron Boe, Kari Hollbrook, Barrett Ward and Tim Sweeney.

Thank you to Bryan Miller and Rich Hollister, who are two of the best leaders I've had.

Thank you, dōTERRA, for being a company that does it right and for the right reasons. Thank you for taking care of my wife while she built a business that ultimately provided an opportunity for our family to help heal people spiritually, emotionally, and financially while living a natural lifestyle—and for me to join her to do my calling full-time! Many thanks to Karina and Gary Sammons for introducing us to dōTERRA and being amazing friends.

Peggy and Dave Smith, Betsy and Paul Holmes, Laura and Shawn King, Kristi Zastrow, Roxanne Benton, Keith and Spring Esteppe, Jim and Lara Hicks, Mark and Lori Vaas, Adam and Tami Nuhfer, Jeremey and Annette Jukes, James Bybee, Roger and Carol-Ann Mendoza, and so many other dōTERRA wellness advocates who have supported Erin and me along the way—thank you for your friendship.

Thank you to the members of Share. Lead. Inspire. You are the highlight of my week and some of my biggest cheerleaders. Your support has meant the world to me as I wrote this book.

Thank you to Rooted Essentials, my adopted team in Charleston, South Carolina. Tiffany, Janel, Christy, and Jessica, you are building something special in the low country, and I am proud of you. Keep changing lives.

Thank you so much, Todd Ackerman. You are one of the best dads and friends I know. Thank you for our friendship, our chats, and your generosity. Working on this book while sitting in your Adirondack camp in Piseco, New York, was a highlight of this journey.

Chris Rawlins, who is a STARfish in every sense of the word, thank you for our friendship, the morning prayers together, and helping me to see things in a different light.

Joel Harrington, who added humor and reality to law school, I'm thankful for our friendship, and I look forward to eating "lobsta" with you in Maine.

A huge thank-you to Team Pure Healthy Essentials. I am so proud of all of you. Your passion, energy, and enthusiasm is contagious. We would not be where we are without you. Thank you all for being part of our family.

Thank you to my Zoweh friends. You do a great thing, and I'm honored to be doing life with you all.

Thank you to Bob Hartig and Frank Gutbrod for working with me to edit and design the book on such a short deadline. I could not have done this without either of you. Looking forward to the next one!

To Mom and Dad, who were always there when I didn't know where I was! You are two STARfish who will go down in the STARfish Hall of Fame.

Finally, thank you to my family. To my three young men, Caleb, Spencer, and Thomas: You have what it takes. I love you. And yes, we will get a farm and an RV!

Erin, you are the greatest STARfish I know and an even better friend and wife. Thank you for your patience and willingness not only to put up with me, but to do double duty while I completed one of my dreams.

Books to Read

- The Bible
- *The Ragamuffin Gospel*—Brennen Manning
- *Mere Christianity*—C.S. Lewis
- *Golf's Sacred Journey*—David L. Cook
- *It's Your Call*—Gary Barkalow
- *Heart of a Warrior*—Michael Thompson
- *Wild at Heart*—John Eldridge
- *Captivating*—Stasi Eldridge
- *Love and Respect*—Dr. Emerson Eggerichs
- *The Greatest Salesman in the World*—Og Mandino
- *7 Habits of Highly Effective People*—Stephen Covey
- *How to Win Friends and Influence People*—Dale Carnegie
- *The Magic of Thinking Big*—David Schwartz
- *4 Arguments for the Elimination of Television*—Jerry Mander
- *The Common Denominator of Success*—Albert Gray
- *The Rich Dad's Cashflow Quadrant*—Robert Kiyosaki
- *Purposed Linked Organization*—Alaina Love and Marc Cugnon
- *Emotional Intelligence*—Daniel Goleman
- *The Millionaire Mind*—Stanley Danko
- *Start with Why*—Simon Sinek

- *Leaders Eat Last*—Simon Sinek
- *The Invisible Touch*—Harry Beckwith
- *Launching a Leadership Revolution*—Orrin Woodward and Chris Brady
- *The Leadership Train*—Orrin Woodward
- *Rascal*—Chris Brady
- *The Compound Effect*—Darren Hardy
- *Last Child in the Woods: Saving Our Children from Nature Deficit Disorder*—Richard Louv